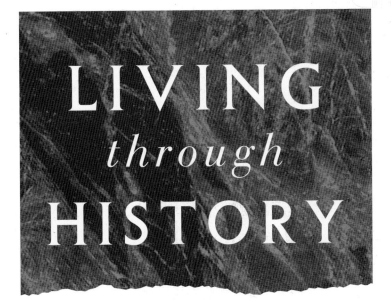

LIVING *through* HISTORY

Black Peoples of the Americas

Nigel Kelly, Rosemary Rees
and Jane Shuter

Heinemann

Heinemann is an imprint of Pearson Education Limited,
a company incorporated in England and Wales, having
its registered office at Edinburgh Gate, Harlow, Essex, CM20 2JE.
Registered company number: 872828

Heinemann is a registered trademark of Pearson Education Limited

First published 1998

09

13

British Library cataloguing in Publication data for this title is available from the British Library.

ISBN: 978 0 435309 91 6

Designed and produced by Dennis Fairey and Associates Ltd.

Illustrated by Sally Artz, John James, Sally Launder, Arthur Phillips, Keith Richmond and Stephen Wisdom.

Photographic acknowledgements

The authors and publisher would like to thank the following for permission to reproduce photographs:

Ancient Art & Architecture Collection/ Ronald Sheridan: 2.1B
Associated Press: 5.6A
Associated Press/Topham: 6.2C
Ida Berman, New York: 5.8B
BFI Stills: 5.2D
Bridgeman Art Library: 2.3A, 3.4B
British Museum: 2.2A
Chicago Historical Society: 3.5A, 5.5A
Corbis-Bettmann: p. 29, 4.1B, 4.3B, 5.1A, 5.2B, 5.3A

Corbis-Bettmann/UPI: 3.4E, 5.1C, 5.2C, 5.3D, p. 52, 6.2B
Corcoran Gallery of Art, Washington DC: 4.4B
Denver Public Library: p. 8
Mary Evans Picture Library: 2.2C
The Granger Collection, New York: 4.3C
Kansas Collection, University of Kansas: p. 7
Library of Congress, Washington DC: 5.4C
Magnum Photos/Bruce Davidson: 6.1C
Magnum Photos/Danny Lyon: 5.8C
Menil Collection, Houston: 2.4B
Nebraska State Historical Society: p. 9
Peter Newark's Pictures: 1.2B, C, 3.6A, 4.2B
New Haven Colony Historical Society: 3.4D
New York Historical Society: 4.2A
Nickelodeon Television: 6.3B
Popperfoto: 5.4A
Popperfoto/Reuters/Fabrizio Bensch: p60
Charmain Reading, New York: 6.1D
Roger-Viollet: 3.4C
Schomburg Center for Research in Black Culture, New York: 2.3B, 3.2A, 4.4A
Worldwide Photos/Birmingham Public Library/Birmingham News, Alabama: 5.7B

The publishers have made evey effort to trace copyright holders of material in this book. Any omissions will be rectified in subsequent printings if notice is given to the publisher.

Printed in China (CTPS/13)

CONTENTS

Who are we studying?

This study looks at the history of the black people of the Americas, from their roots through to the present day.

It has been impossible to cover every event in such a long history, or to cover every part of the Americas – North America, South America and the West Indies. We have concentrated on the lives of black people in the United States. We have also mixed the overall story of what happened with more detailed glimpses into the lives of real people. It is important to remember that not everyone would have had the same experiences.

What's in a name?

At different times black people have referred to themselves in different ways. There was a time when 'black' was seen as insulting, while 'Negro' was not. At other times 'Negro' has been seen as insulting. We have used 'black people' throughout the book. This is the most acceptable term to black people now. In the sources we have left the words the writers used.

Most black people came to America from Africa as slaves. This map shows the route the slave ships took.

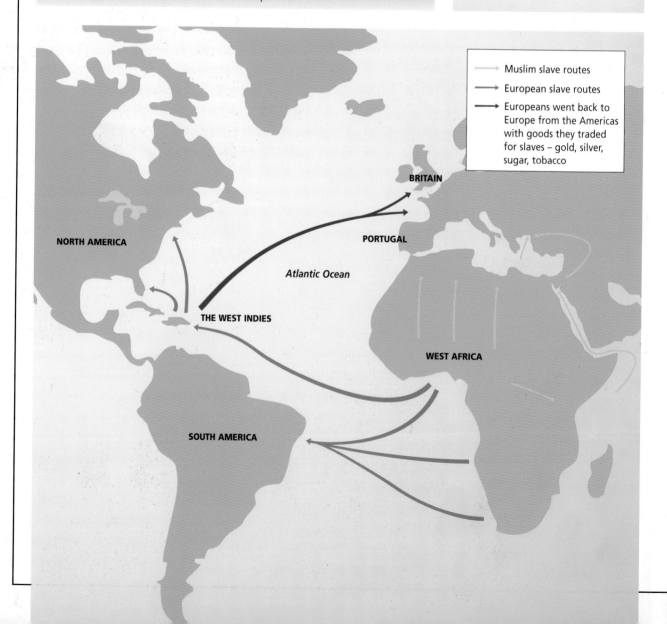

Muslim slave routes

European slave routes

Europeans went back to Europe from the Americas with goods they traded for slaves – gold, silver, sugar, tobacco

BRITAIN

NORTH AMERICA

PORTUGAL

Atlantic Ocean

THE WEST INDIES

WEST AFRICA

SOUTH AMERICA

Ideas

Although this book covers hundreds of years, there are some ideas that run all the way through. These are the ideas of freedom and equality.

- **Freedom:** At first, black people in the Americas had to fight against slavery. Most were brought from Africa to the Americas as slaves. They were bought and sold, just like any other property. Some managed to buy their freedom. But very few free blacks were treated as equals by white people. They were often kidnapped and sold into slavery.

- **Equality:** Once slavery was stopped, in 1865, there was a chance for black people to become equal to white people – to have the same voting rights, the same education and the same chances of getting a job. But they came up against strong **racial prejudice**. White people, even those who had opposed slavery and had treated black people well, did not see black people as equals.

Source A

This letter was written by Abraham Camp in 1818. It could just as easily have been written 100 years earlier or later.

I am a free man of colour. I, my family and many of the people in the black settlement where I live beside the Wabash River are all willing to leave America, if a way can be found. We love this country and its liberties, if we could share an equal right in them. But our freedom is partial, and we have no hope it will ever be otherwise, so we would rather be gone, to Africa or to some other place.

Things to think about

As you read this book, ask yourself:

- Are black people legally free?
- Are black people truly free to choose?
- Are black people being treated as equals?
- Are things better than they were before?
- Are things good enough?

Why did white people deny black people equality?

They are not as clever as whites. They need telling what to do, like children.

They are lazy. Without us, they sit around all day.

They are dangerous. Give them half a chance and they will rob you, or worse.

We're just ordinary people. Give us a chance.

1.2 INVISIBLE PEOPLE?

We are going to begin our study of black people by looking at the way they have been left out of many history books, using the example of black people in the West. The story of the West, as told by white historians, storytellers and film-makers used to give a very biased picture. White settlers and cowboys were the heroes. Native American Indians were the warlike villains who killed peaceful white settlers. Black people were simply ignored.

In reality, there were many black people in the West. There were black slaves, free blacks, black cowboys, black outlaws, black farmers and black miners. There were towns (such as Deerfield, Colorado, and Langston, Oklahoma) that had totally black populations. Just like the whites, some blacks were rich, some poor, some good and some bad. And just as happened everywhere, some blacks were treated well, but most were not. Here are the stories of a few of them.

Source A

Carter Woodson, launching Negro History Week in 1926, told his audience:

If a race has no history, it becomes unimportant in the eyes of the world.

Where was 'the West'? The settlement of the western states.

Washington 1853 [1889]

Oregon 1848 [1859]

Idaho 1863 [1890]

Montana 1864 [1889]

North Dakota 1861 [1889]

Minnesota 1849 [1858]

South Dakota 1861 [1889]

Wyoming 1868 [1890]

Iowa 1838 [1846]

Nevada 1850 [1896]

Utah 1850 [1896]

Colorado 1861 [1876]

Nebraska 1859 [1867]

Kansas 1854 [1861]

Missouri 1805 [1821]

California 1850

Arizona 1863 [1912]

New Mexico 1850 [1912]

Oklahoma 1890 [1907]

Arkansas 1819 [1836]

Louisiana 1804 [1812]

Texas 1845

First United States

Added later

1805 Date of settlement

[1821] Date became a state

Law and order

Black towns elected their own officials; their mayors and sheriffs were black. But there were black sheriffs in other towns, too. This man was sheriff of Abilene, a big cattle town in the West.

Source B

Black and white miners, digging for gold.

ALVIN COFFEY

Alvin Coffey started out from St Louis on 2 April 1849. He was a slave taken west by his master, who went to California as part of the rush to look for gold. Coffey wrote of the journey and their first few months there:

One of us died of the cholera and more were dying every day. We drove all the faster to get out of its reach. We got across the plains to Fort Laramie by 16 June. There were a good many people ahead of us; we found things they left along the way, including bacon. A great many cattle died crossing to Black Rock over the desert. We crossed the South Pass on 4 July. The ice next morning was thick as a dinner plate. On 15 October we began our first digging. We dug and dug till the first of November. That night it began to rain and it rained and snowed pretty much all winter. Our tent barely kept us dry. There were eight to twelve of us in each camp. We cut down pine trees and built a cabin. It was a whole week before we had a cabin to keep ourselves dry.

Over several years, Coffey made $5000 for his master and, by working nights for himself, $700 towards buying his freedom. Then his master stole the money and sold Coffey. Coffey started all over again. But he earned enough money to buy freedom for himself and his wife and three children, too. By the 1860s the Coffeys were all free.

Black cowboys

About one out of three cowboys in the West was black. At the time, this was the job where black men had the best chance of equality with whites. Their pay and living conditions were exactly the same as for white cowboys, although they were less likely to be given the most important jobs. Nat Love, a famous black cowboy, later wrote the story of his life in the West. He says he was treated as an equal by everyone, black or white, outlaw or sheriff. When he had to stop working as a cowboy, he ended up working on the railways.

Even as late as 1910, when this picture was taken, there were cowboys in the West. Many were black.

ISOM DART

Not all black settlers in the West were law abiding. Isom Dart, born a slave in 1849, moved West after 1865. He became a cattle thief. Once, his gang was ambushed while burying a friend. Dart escaped by throwing himself in the grave and not getting out until night fell. Eventually, in 1900, he was shot.

Things to do

1 a List some images of the American West you have seen – films, cartoons, adverts, books and so on.
   b Put a tick next to each image on the list where black people were included.

2 a Read **Black cowboys**. About how many cowboys in the West were black?
   b Before you read this book, did you know there were any?

3 Read Source A.

   Would Carter Woodson think it was important to trace the history of black people in the West? Explain why.

4 a What sorts of black people went west?
   b Why did they go?
   c What sorts of work did they do?

Making their own way

Black women mostly went west with their families or owners. But once in the West they could find themselves making their way on their own – either by choice or by necessity.

BIDDY MASON

Biddy Mason was taken to California in 1849 by her master, who was looking for gold. Biddy herded the cattle on the journey. In 1856 her master went home but Biddy Mason and her three daughters stayed. She worked hard and made enough money to buy some land. She made more money, invested it and bought more land. She gave the land away for building schools, churches and homes. She helped the poor, people in jail and people struck by disaster. She died in 1891.

Settlers

Many newly freed black slave families moved west to start a new life farming. This is the Speese family, outside their home in Custer County, Nebraska, in 1888. There was no wood on the Plains, so settlers had to make their homes out of turf (called 'sod'). The houses were called 'soddies', the settlers 'sodbusters'. These black sodbusters have a bigger than average home, so they must be doing well. They also have two buggies and a wind-powered water pump.

MARY FIELDS

Mary Fields was born a slave in Tennessee in the 1830s. She went west in the 1880s, to work at the St Peter's Mission in Cascade, Montana. She got into a shoot-out with one of the men there, and lost her job. She ran a restaurant, but it failed. In 1895, in her sixties, she drove a stagecoach and delivered the mail. At seventy, she opened a laundry. She spent most of her time in the saloon. One day she saw a customer who had not paid his bill, chased him down the street and knocked him out. *His bill is settled*, she said. Mary Fields died in 1914.

The history of the black people of the Americas can be traced back to Africa, to the first human ancestor, born in Africa some 200,000 years ago. Africa is huge. In the years before white people landed on its coast, the continent was divided into many kingdoms, with a large number of different peoples. They were not, as many white people later saw them, either wild savages or simple, noble people in need of education and care.

West Africa

Most black Americans can trace their roots to West Africa. Evidence that has survived from the time shows that the people in early West African kingdoms were rich, skilled and cultured.

Some early West African kingdoms

Nok	powerful in about 500 BC
Ghana	powerful in about 1000 AD
Mali	powerful in about 1300 AD
Ife	flourishing at the same time as Mali, but existing outside it
Benin	flourishing at the same time as Mali, but existing outside it
Songhai	powerful in the 1400s AD

Source A

In 1107 an Arab historian, Al-Bakri, described the king of Ghana, Tenkamenin.

He can call on more than 200,000 warriors in battle. When he meets his people to listen to their complaints, he sits in a great tent around which stand horses covered in cloth of gold. He is guarded by ten men with shields and gold-handled swords. The princes of his empire stand with him, with gold plaited in their hair. Even his dogs have collars of gold and silver.

Some kingdoms and tribes of West Africa in about 1400.

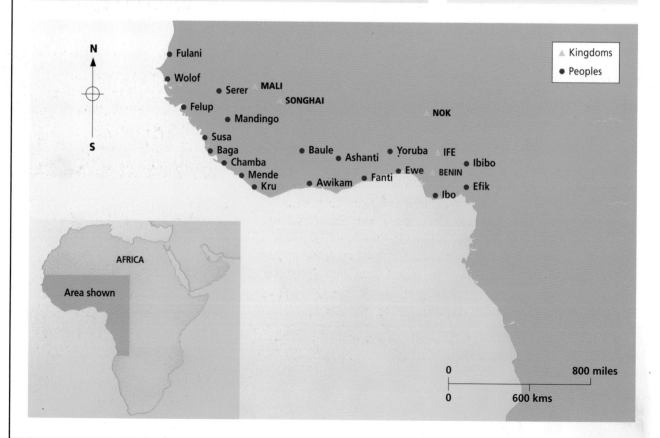

Contact with other countries

West African kingdoms had contact with other African peoples and with the **Islamic** Arabs, who controlled parts of North Africa. These contacts took two main forms: war and trade.

War

Various African kingdoms fought each other at various times. Their warriors took prisoners in battle, and these prisoners were often made slaves. A member of the Benin people described their slaves: *They do no more work than any other person, even their master. Their food, lodgings and clothing are almost the same, although they are not allowed to eat with free men.*

Trade

The first people the West Africans had contact with were the Arabs, who traded salt, spices and books for gold and slaves. The Arabs also brought with them their religion, Islam, which several kingdoms accepted as their own. Others kept their old religions. These varied, but their beliefs usually included respect for ancestors and the worship of some form of Supreme Being.

A brass head made by the Ife people. The Ife sent people to the kingdom of Benin, to teach them how to make brass sculptures like these. The people of Benin later became famous for their brass sculptures.

African slavery before 1440

Slavery existed in Africa before white people arrived. But it was a very different sort of slavery than was to come later.

- **Most slaves were people captured in battle**. Temporary slavery, for a set number of years, was a punishment for some crimes in some kingdoms.

- **Slaves were treated differently in different kingdoms**. In most kingdoms, slaves worked for the people who captured them until their own people paid to free them. In some cases they could work to buy their freedom. Other slaves were sold to Arab slave dealers, who took them back across the desert and sold them on. But the Islamic religion taught kindness to slaves. It even taught that it was a good deed to let them go.

- **Children of slaves did not automatically become slaves**. So slavery was a temporary state that people could escape from.

Things to do

1 What evidence is there that West African kingdoms before 1440:

   a had an organised system of government?
   b had a high level of skills?

2 How was slavery built into their way of life?

In 1444 Portuguese explorers discovered the west coast of Africa. They captured black people from the villages near their landing place and took them back to Portugal. The European slave trade had begun.

Slow beginnings

At first, this slave trade was very like earlier slavery. Some black people were taken back to Portugal, where they mixed freely with white people, working with them and marrying them. Their slavery was not permanent, and they could work for their freedom. The white Portuguese saw people in the rich kingdoms like Benin as people to trade with, not as savages.

Changing needs

But then the Americas were discovered in the 1490s. Black people were part of the crews of almost all the Spanish and Portuguese expeditions to this new land. As white people began to settle there, it became clear that they could only make homes in this new wilderness by a lot of work. At first they used **indentured servants**. But when they started mining in South America, or farming sugar or tobacco in North America, they needed many more workers. There were not enough indentured servants to do the work. White people began to use the local Indians as slaves. They also began to look for slaves from other places. So the slave trade with Africa began, and with it a whole new sort of slavery.

Source A

A bronze figure of a European soldier. It was made by the Benin, using the technique of casting bronze that they learned from the Ife people.

Indentured servants

Indentured servants were people who signed an agreement to work without pay for several years (usually seven) in return for having their crossing to America paid for. The person who paid this had a right to their work for seven years and could sell it on to anyone. Although there was a time limit, indentured servants were like slaves, because they could be sold.

Things to do

1 a Look at Sources A and C carefully. What did white people have to help them control black people?
  b Why did white people feel they could just take other people to use as slaves?

2 Read **African slavery before 1440** on page 11 and **African slavery after 1440** on page 13.

  Draw a '**before** and **after**' diagram to show how slavery in the two periods differed.

The first black Americans

By 1502 the Spanish were using black slaves in South America. The first black North Americans were not slaves. The Governor of Virginia, John Rolfe, recorded their arrival in 1619: *About the last of August came in a Dutch man-of-war that sold us 20 Negroes.* The Africans Rolfe's people bought became part of the indentured servant system already set up in the colony. They learned trades to support themselves when they were free. These first black settlers progressed through their own efforts, just like indentured whites. They had black servants of their own, and in some places they could vote.

Quick change

But inequality crept in quickly. The need for a lot of workers tilted the balance against black people. Laws made in the colonies no longer applied equally. In 1639 the laws of Maryland protected the rights of *all Christian inhabitants, excepting slaves.* In the early 1700s states took away the rights of black people to vote and have an education.

African slavery after 1440

Slavery changed when white people became involved. At first no one (including black people who sold other blacks) realised what would happen. The main changes were:

- **It became a profitable trade.** White slave traders needed lots of slaves. So people were captured to be made slaves, rather than becoming slaves through war or as a punishment.
- **It became an overseas trade.** The distances and the difficulty of the journey were huge. Slaves had no chance of getting back home.
- **It became a way of life, not a temporary state.** Children whose parents were slaves were seen as slaves too.
- **The way that slaves were treated changed for the worse.** Because slavery was no longer a temporary state, and because there were so many slaves, they were seen by their white owners as less than human. This meant they were often treated very badly.

Source B

The Dutchman Hans Staden visited Brazil in the 1540s. He wrote this account of the Spanish and their slaves.

When they ran out of native slaves the Spanish began to use blacks from Guinea. At first they made them work in the gold and silver mines. As these have run out they now use them on sugar plantations. Some Spaniards are not just cruel to their slaves, they are very cruel. They torture them for the least wrongdoing. Some have managed to escape, and have become very fierce and numerous. While I was there, Hispaniola saw a big rebellion, and many think it will fall into the hands of these blacks entirely.

An illustration from a 1592 edition of Hans Staden's book about his travels.

Source C

2.3 OLAUDAH EQUIANO

The slave trade to the Americas became big business very quickly. In 1700 there were about 250,000 people in the parts of North America controlled by the British. By 1776 there were 2,500,000. Of these, 500,000 were black. Some of these black people were born in America. Some of them were free. But most of them were people brought over from Africa and sold as slaves. Here is the story of one of them.

OLAUDAH EQUIANO

Olaudah Equiano was born in Benin in 1745. He and his sister were kidnapped when he was eleven years old. From his story, it seems that kidnapping by other tribes was always a danger. The children were separated, and only saw each other once more. Olaudah was sold several times on his way to the coast. Once he was bought as a slave for a boy of his own age and spent about two months being treated almost as an equal. But then he was sold on again. Eventually he was taken to America. He was a slave in Barbados, then sold to a planter in Virginia, then to a British ship's captain, then to a merchant in Philadelphia. He bought his freedom when he was twenty-one, worked as a seaman, then settled in England, where he campaigned for the ending of the slave trade. In 1789 he wrote his autobiography. He married a white woman and had two children. He died in 1797.

Olaudah Equiano, painted when he was a free man.

Capture and journey to the coast

Here is part of Olaudah Equiano's story in his own words:

One day, when the adults were out working and my sister and I were left to mind the house, two men and a woman got over our wall and seized us both and ran off with us to the nearest wood. In the morning, we left the wood and took to a road. I saw some people in the distance and called out for help, but my captors tied me up and stuffed me into a sack. The next day my sister and I were separated. I was sold here and there, then moved on. In about seven months we reached the coast. The first thing I saw was the sea, and a slave ship, anchored, waiting for its cargo.

I was taken on board and handled roughly, by the crew, to see if I was healthy. Their skin was a different colour from ours. Their skin, their long hair, the language they spoke, all made me think I was in a world of bad spirits who would kill me. I looked around the deck and saw many black people of every kind, chained together. I no longer doubted my fate and, overcome with horror, fainted. When I came to, the black people who had brought me on board talked to me. I asked if we were to be eaten by the white men with horrible looks, red faces and long hair. They said not. Soon after they left and I was abandoned to despair.

The crossing

I now saw myself robbed of any chance of returning home. I was soon put under the deck. There was such an awful stink as I had never smelt before. Everyone was crying and I was soon too unhappy to eat or wish for anything but death. When I refused food two white men tied me up and flogged me. I had never been treated like this before. Despite the fact I could not swim, I would have jumped over the side; but there were nets there and I could not. The crew watched those of us who were on deck very closely to stop us leaping into the water. After a while I found some people from my own country and asked them what would happen to us. They told me that we would be carried to the white people's country, to work for them.

I was still fearful, because the white people were so savage. I had never before seen such cruelty, not only to us blacks, but to whites also – I saw one flogged to death and just tossed overboard.

The smell below decks was so bad that some of us were let up onto the deck. Once, we were all forced below decks. The heat and the number of people (when all below we scarcely had room to turn around) was suffocating. We all sweated, and that smell added to the rest, which caused many to fall sick and die. Some children even fell into the big tubs we had to use as toilets and nearly died. The shrieks of the women and the groans of the dying made it unbelievably horrifying. I was lucky in that I spent most of the time on deck, and was considered too young to wear chains.

Source B

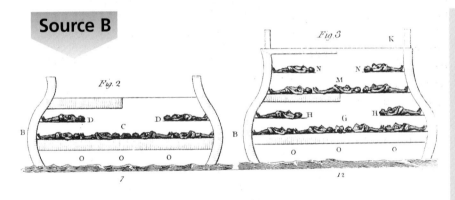

How the slave ship *Brookes* was loaded in the 1830s. Conditions were so bad that the slave traders expected a quarter of their cargo, if not more, to die on the crossing. The Portuguese for slave ship, *tumbeiros*, was also their word for coffin.

Things to do

Read Olaudah Equiano's story.

1 What did Olaudah think was going to happen when he was first taken on board?

2 Describe in your own words what it was like below decks.

3 Compare your description to Source B. In what way do they agree?

4 What does Olaudah's story tell you that Source B cannot?

5 Which gives the best idea of what conditions were like on a slave ship? Why?

6 Why did the slave traders use: **a** nets **b** chains?

The first stop for most African slaves was the West Indies. Some never left, others were moved on to North or South America. The West Indies was where a slave was turned from a person into a possession. There were several steps to this, including splitting up families and friends, changing people's names and setting black people against each other. Some black people had to become Christian and were not allowed to speak their own language.

What's your name?

Slaves were not called by their own name. They were given a name when they arrived in the West Indies, but owners could change the names of their slaves as often as they wanted. So Olaudah Equiano was called Michael, then Jacob, then Gustavus. When he tried to keep the name Jacob, *he still called me Gustavus. When I refused to answer to it, which at first I did, he hit me, so at last I gave in.*

An 1849 painting of a disobedient slave being whipped. It is unlikely that the slaves would have looked as healthy and unscarred as these, or that the **planter's** wife and child would have been there to watch.

Source A

Olaudah Equiano tells of his arrival in the West Indies.

We arrived at Barbados. Many merchants and planters came aboard. They looked us over and put us into groups, and made us jump about to see how fit we were. Next day we were taken to the merchant's yard and shut up together, like sheep in a pen. We were not there long before we were sold. At the beating of a drum the buyers rushed to buy the groups they wanted. So friends and relations were separated, never to see each other again. The brothers who came over together in my ship were all sold separately.

Source B

Verdier 1849.

From person to possession

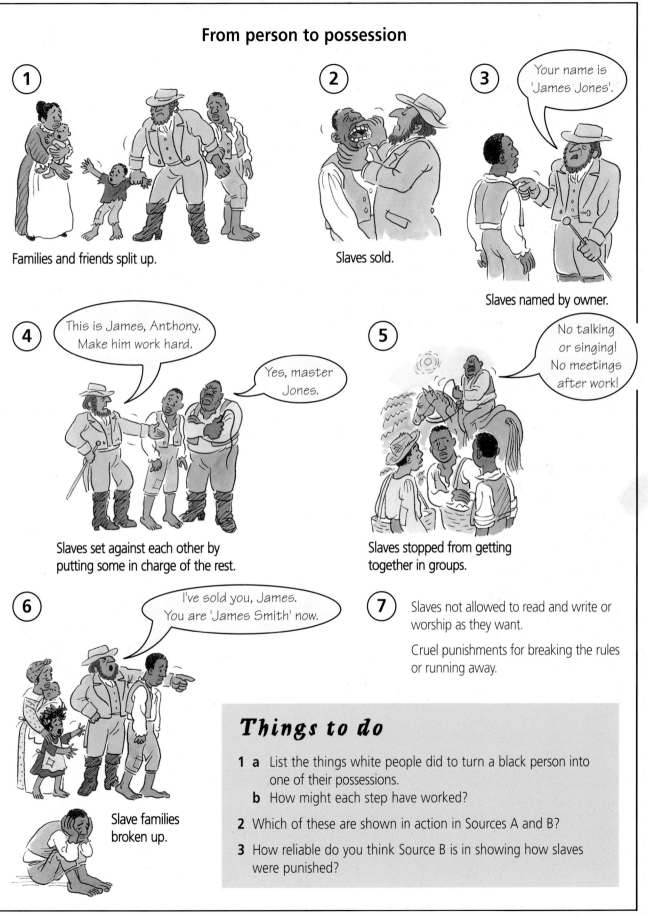

1 Families and friends split up.

2 Slaves sold.

3 "Your name is 'James Jones'."

Slaves named by owner.

4 "This is James, Anthony. Make him work hard."

"Yes, master Jones."

Slaves set against each other by putting some in charge of the rest.

5 "No talking or singing! No meetings after work!"

Slaves stopped from getting together in groups.

6 "I've sold you, James. You are 'James Smith' now."

Slave families broken up.

7 Slaves not allowed to read and write or worship as they want.

Cruel punishments for breaking the rules or running away.

Things to do

1 a List the things white people did to turn a black person into one of their possessions.

 b How might each step have worked?

2 Which of these are shown in action in Sources A and B?

3 How reliable do you think Source B is in showing how slaves were punished?

In 1776 the people living in British colonies (land owned by the British in America) began a war to become independent of Britain. A Declaration of Independence was read to representatives from all the colonies. Among other things, it accused the British king of *violating the rights of life and liberty in the persons of a distant people who had never offended him.* This was a declaration against slavery itself. But representatives of the southern colonies, where slavery was most widespread, refused to sign if this sentence was included. The colonies had to be united to beat the British, so it was dropped.

Source A

Part of the Declaration of Independence, 4 July 1776.

We hold these truths to be self-evident, that all men are created equal, that God has given them rights which cannot be taken away. Among these are life, liberty and the pursuit of happiness.

Fighting for liberty

Black people took part in the early uprisings against the British. But it soon became clear that the rebels did not want black people in their army. Their general, George Washington, made a speech refusing to let black people fight, even if they had been in the army before.

The British, on the other hand, asked black people to join them in return for their own freedom. About 1000 slaves joined the British. Washington now changed his mind. He said black men who had previously served in the army could re-enlist. About 5000 black men fought on the American side. Most of them were free northern blacks, rather than runaway slaves. Many of them were later praised for their bravery in battle.

CRISPUS ATTICUS

Crispus Atticus, a runaway slave, was one of the first Americans to die fighting the British. He was killed in the Boston Massacre of 1770, an early outbreak of violence between the British and Americans. As Source C shows, the whole city mourned Crispus and the others.

Source B

In 1791 a free black man, Benjamin Banneker, wrote this to Thomas Jefferson (who wrote the Declaration of Independence, yet owned slaves).

Sir, let me remind you of when the British were trying to control you. You spoke very clearly about how you were entitled to liberty. It is pitiful to think that, while you were convinced that God made people equal, you keep so many of my people in captivity. You are, it seems, guilty of that most criminal act that you say you hate in others.

Source C

A newspaper report of the funeral of men killed fighting against the British in 1770.

Last Thursday, the bodies of Samuel Grey, Samuel Maverick, James Caldwell and Crispus Atticus – the unhappy victims who fell in the bloody massacre of last Monday evening – were carried to their grave.

Most of the shops in town were shut and all the bells were rung solemnly, as were those in the neighbouring towns. The procession began to move between 4 and 5 o'clock in the afternoon, followed by many people of all ranks, their relations and friends. At the back was a long train of carriages belonging to the gentry of the town. The distress and sorrow on every face and the solemnity of the whole funeral are beyond description.

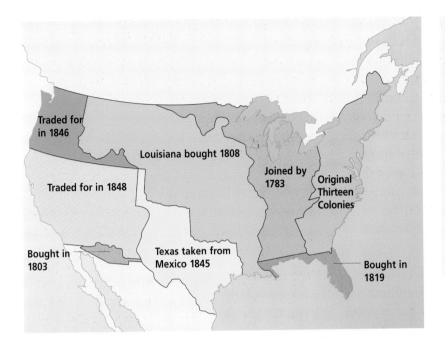

This map shows how the United States grew. In 1808 the biggest single area, Louisiana (bought from the French for about 10p an acre!), was added all at once, more than doubling the size of the nation. The federal government could have banned slavery here. Instead, when Louisiana was divided into states, each state could make its own decision about slavery.

Map labels:
- Traded for in 1846
- Louisiana bought 1808
- Joined by 1783
- Original Thirteen Colonies
- Traded for in 1848
- Bought in 1803
- Texas taken from Mexico 1845
- Bought in 1819

A united nation?

The thirteen colonies became thirteen states, each with its own government. But the thirteen states together also set up, by the **Constitution** of 1787, a **Federal government**. Each state now had two representatives in the federal senate. How many representatives of each state there were in the lower house depended on the size of its population. In counting up the people in the state, black people (most of whom could not vote) counted as three fifths of a person. Each state made its own laws about things not in the Constitution.

If the Constitution had abolished slavery, this would have applied across all the states. But the southern states dug in their heels and refused to allow it. They did, however, agree to a clause in the Constitution that after twenty years (in 1808) the slave trade could be abolished. But they made sure the Constitution also said that slaves (whom it called 'persons held to service or labour') were to be returned to their owners if they escaped. Otherwise, the states were left to make their own, varying laws about slavery.

Source D

In 1852 the people of Rochester asked Frederick Douglass, a free black man, to give the Fourth of July speech, celebrating Independence Day. His reaction was:

Pardon me, and allow me to ask, but why am I called to speak here today? This Fourth of July is yours, not mine. You may rejoice, I must mourn. To drag a man in chains to the temple of liberty and call upon him to rejoice with you – are you mocking me? Over your joy I hear the mournful wail of millions, whose chains, heavy yesterday, are made more unbearable by celebrations all around the nation today.

Things to do

1 Why might some people in America in 1776 have been suprised by what is said in Source A?

2 Do you think the Constitution set up after the War of Independence was really based on what is said in Source A?

3 Re-write Frederick Douglass' speech (Source D) in your own words.

North and South

Over time, the position of black people in the North and South of the USA became different. This was not because northerners were kinder, but because they did not need as many slaves. At first, slaves were needed to grow crops on **plantations** in both the North and the South. The plantations were quite small. In 1790 the average plantation in the North had about thirteen slaves. In the South the average was twenty-two, but there were some big plantations with over 100 slaves.

The demand for cotton rose, so the southern plantations, where it was grown, became bigger. In 1793 a machine was invented to process cotton faster, so even more was grown. Plantation owners depended on slave labour. The tobacco industry in the North was becoming less important. Slaves were not as vital.

Many northern states began 'gradual emancipation' – freeing children of existing slaves when they were twenty-one. Because the owners had not had to buy these slaves, they accepted losing them.

Free and unfree

Most black people in the North were free by 1860. In the South, 89 per cent of black people were slaves. So was the North a better place for black people? Yes, in that a free black person living and working in a northern town was better off than a black slave in the South. But freedom did not mean equality. There was racial prejudice in the North. Black people competed with white people for work. This led to tensions that did not exist in the South. Freedom did not give black people the vote, or an equal education.

Free did not mean safe, either. The slave trade was big business. It did not take slave dealers long to see that Africa was not the only source of black slaves. They could go north, kidnap black people there, take them south and sell them into slavery.

The slave states in 1860. Many northerners objected to slave states joining the United States. The Missouri Compromise (1820) abolished slavery in states north of a certain line on the map. In 1854 this was changed. People in new states could make their own decisions about slavery.

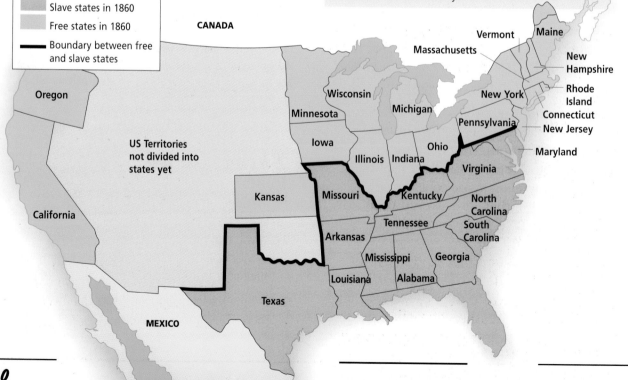

Slave states in 1860
Free states in 1860
Boundary between free and slave states

CANADA

Oregon

Wisconsin
Minnesota
Michigan
New York
Vermont
Massachusetts
Maine
New Hampshire
Rhode Island
Connecticut
New Jersey
Pennsylvania
Maryland

US Territories not divided into states yet

Iowa
Illinois
Indiana
Ohio
Virginia

Kansas
Missouri
Kentucky
North Carolina

California
Tennessee
South Carolina

Arkansas
Mississippi
Alabama
Georgia

Louisiana

Texas

MEXICO

THE CASE OF SOLOMON NORTHRUP

Solomon Northrup was born in 1808 in New York State, the son of a freed slave. By 1838 Solomon and his wife and children were living in Saratoga Springs. One of the ways in which he made money was by playing the violin. In March 1841, two white men offered him work in their travelling circus: good wages for several weeks' work. He went with them. They took him as far as Washington, where they drugged his drink one night.

Northrup said that he woke *alone, in utter darkness, and in chains.* A slave dealer came for him. *I told him I was a free man, with a wife and children who were in Saratoga, also free. Again and again I insisted that I was no man's slave, and insisted on his taking off my chains at once.* Northrup was beaten over and over again, until, fearing for his life, he said he was a slave. There were escaped slaves and free men in the group the slave trader took by boat to New Orleans, where Northrup was sold. He was bought by William Ford, a planter, who was a kind master. But Ford fell into debt and sold some slaves (Northrup included) to pay his debt off. Northrup was bought by a carpenter, John Tibbet, who was cruel. Northrup ran away, through the swamps, with Tibbet in hot pursuit. He went to the Fords, who persuaded Tibbet to hire him out. He was then sold on to Epps, a cotton planter. In 1852, a man called Bass came to the Epps plantation. Northrup trusted him, and told his story. Bass helped him write home. A lawyer was sent to find him, and by January 1853 Northrup was home. Most kidnapped free men never got home. Northrup died four months after his return.

The price of a slave

Slaves were auctioned off. Prices varied, depending on who was at the auction and how much they wanted a slave. Here are some average prices of a young black man listed in planters' accounts:

1800	$70
1840	$600
1850	$1500
1860	$2000

Prices could be far higher. Zamba (who described a sale in 1800) was sold before the auction for $600. The prices of those sold at auction ranged from $250 to $450.

Source A

$1200 TO 1250 DOLLARS! FOR NEGROES!!

THE undersigned wishes to purchase a large lot of NEGROES for the New Orleans market. I will pay $1200 to $1250 for No. 1 young men, and $850 to $1000 for No. 1 young women. In fact I will pay more for likely

NEGROES,

Than any other trader in Kentucky. My office is adjoining the Broadway Hotel, on Broadway, Lexington, Ky., where I or my Agent can always be found.

WM. F. TALBOTT.

LEXINGTON, JULY 2, 1853.

Things to do

1 Make a list of the slave states in the USA in 1860.

2 Why did slavery grow in the southern states, not the North?

3 Read the story of Solomon Northrup.

   a How long was Northrup a slave?

   b How many different owners did he have?

   c Why do you think Northrup did not tell 'kind' planter Ford that he was a free man?

The demand for slaves was high. Slave traders advertised to buy slaves, not sell them! They did not ask too many questions about where the 'slaves' brought to them came from.

3.3 SHOULD SLAVERY BE ABOLISHED?

The debate over whether or not slavery should be abolished raged for many years. The first abolitionists (people to say that slavery was absolutely wrong and should be abolished) were from the Quaker religious movement. As early as 1688, Quakers were speaking out against slavery. In 1693 they published the first anti-slavery document. Anti-slavery feeling continued to rise. The formal separation of the states into 'free' and 'slave' states (even if there were laws about returning runaway slaves) drew the battle line. When the separation was first made by the Missouri Compromise of 1820, the representative for Georgia said:
You have kindled a fire which all the waters of the ocean cannot put out, which only seas of blood can extinguish.

What did the abolitionists do?

Abolitionists – black and white, male and female – wrote pamphlets, made speeches against slavery and even published their own newspapers. Preachers from black and white churches spoke against slavery in church and in the streets. But abolitionists were not one big, united group. They held various views on abolition. Sometimes they argued as hotly with each other as they did with supporters of slavery. Some abolitionists tried to fight the view of many white people that black people were inferior. They set up schools for black people. This was not always welcomed, even in the North. In the South there were cries of outrage that people in other states should dare to tell them what to do.

Slavery is wrong. Black people are just like anyone else. They should have equal chances.

What a silly idea! They should be free; but they are not equal. They are like simple children.

Free them and send them back home to Africa. They belong there. Staying here will cause problems.

Free them and train them to work for us. They will be loyal and hard-working and grateful. But they need to be told what to do.

Free us, give us a chance of equal education and jobs, then you will see what we can do.

Different abolitionist views.

Slavery is wrong

Source A

This is part of *American Slavery As It Is*, a book published by the preacher Theodore Dwight Weld in 1839.

There are 2,700,000 persons in America, men, women and children, in slavery. They were made slaves, and are held there by force and fear. And all for no crime! Is slavery good, bad, or neither? You have a family – put them, put yourself, in the place of the slaves, and decide. Every man knows that slavery is a curse. Try him; clank the chains in his ears and tell him they are for him. Give him an hour to prepare his wife and children for slavery! Slave holders talk of treating slaves well, yet rob them of all they can get, of their very selves – their hands and feet; their muscles; their bodies and minds; their time, liberty and earnings; their right to learn.

Yet they want us to believe that their soft hearts ooze so lovingly to these slaves that they keep them well housed and dressed, never work them too hard, never let them go hungry. Are they stupid, or do they think the rest of the world is stupid, to believe this? Slaves are treated like animals. They are overworked, underfed, badly clothed and housed. They do not get enough rest. They are forced to wear chains, iron collars with prongs. They are shut up for weeks altogether. They are made to wear gags that tear their mouths, they have their teeth torn out, they are flogged and have salt rubbed into the cuts. If they run away they are hunted down by dogs, whipped, branded, maimed, mutilated and more. It is not just slaves that tell us this. It is judges, doctors, merchants, preachers – responsible people.

Slavery is right

Source B

This is part of a speech made by the Governor of South Carolina from 1834 to 1836, George McDuffie.

Certain societies and persons in some of the non-slaveholding states have been publishing pamphlets and pictures meant to get our slaves to rise up and kill us all. We need answer only to God for slavery. And slavery clearly has his blessing.

The African Negro is destined by Providence to slavery. It is marked on his skin and by his lack of intelligence and ability to care for himself. They are in all respects inferior to us. They are not able to cope with freedom. People who would free the black race have only to look to those still in Africa to see how much our slaves have gained by their servitude.

Where would they go if they were freed? They could not stay here. We could not live as equals. One group or the other would have to be master. Transportation to Africa is the only answer, and they would lose by it. Our slaves are more comfortable than many who suffer and starve without a master. They work less than people in other countries doing similar work. They eat twice as much and know their masters will care for them, even into old age. Our slaves are cheerful, contented and happy.

The production of cotton depends not on soil, or climate, but on slavery. If slaves were freed cotton production would fall from 1,200,000 bales to 600,000 bales. Little more than two million Negro slaves set at liberty would beggar ten million white men, instantly.

Things to do

1 Read the arguments about whether slavery is right or wrong.

   a Under the headings **Right** and **Wrong** list the points each person makes to support his argument.

   b Alongside each point, write the answer that an opponent of that view would give to it.

2 Read what the representative for Georgia said about the Missouri Compromise in the text on page 22. What did he mean?

Slaves did not just sit quietly and wait for abolitionists to rescue them. They fought back in many different ways.

Passive resistance

Many slaves resisted in non-violent ways, which cut down the profit of the plantations. Their acts of resistance often cleverly used the white view of black people as naturally clumsy and lazy. In this way they might avoid severe punishment. For example, they worked slowly, did their work badly, pretended to be sick and deliberately broke tools or let animals loose.

They also ran away. This was easier to do on the islands of the West Indies, where the runaways could live wild in the mountains or join the pirates who infested that area.

Violent resistance

As early as 1712, in New York, slaves rebelled against their masters. This was a last resort, as rebellion was often doomed to failure. Again, it was easier in the West Indies, where there were far more slaves than whites, and where it was harder for other whites to reach those under attack.

Wherever there was slavery, the slaves resisted in some way. This fed the fears of white slave owners. But they did not react by abolishing slavery, or treating their slaves better. Instead, they were even more oppressive. On these pages and pages 26–7 are some examples of resistance to slavery at different times.

Source A

A visitor to a plantation in 1793 wrote:

The slaves here are very well cared for. They are very lazy and slow. They break tools through clumsiness, though before I came I heard they were a graceful people. They do not seem very grateful for care they are given.

Things to do

Read Source A.

Which of the visitor's criticisms of black people could be evidence of passive resistance?

Harvesting sugar cane in Antigua, in the West Indies, in 1823. The sheer number of slaves, and the fact they needed to be given tools that might be used as weapons, added to white fears.

Source B

Resistance in San Domingo: a success story

The island of San Domingo was half Spanish, half French. Both countries used slaves to grow crops, mainly sugar cane but also cotton and coffee. French San Domingo, in the west of the island, was described as *the worst hell on earth*. Every year, 40,000 slaves arrived from Africa. It was more profitable to buy slaves, work them to death and then replace them, than to keep them alive to breed new slaves. French laws about slaves, which said what they should be fed, how much they should work and how they could be punished, were all ignored. Slaves were badly cared for and overworked. They were beaten, starved, tortured and killed. The death rate for slaves was the highest in the Americas.

Many slaves ran away to the mountains, to live free as best they could. No one knew how many of them there were, but the white planters feared that there were thousands, and that they came secretly to plantations to encourage other slaves to join them or, even worse, to revolt.

In 1789 the people of France rebelled against their king. Their slogan was 'Liberty, equality, brotherhood'. When news of this reached the French colonies, the planters were, quite rightly, scared.

The first group to revolt were the mulattos (people with mixed black and white blood) in 1791. This revolt was crushed. But a slave rebellion, led by a **voodoo** priest called Boukman, also broke out. It was carefully planned. Slaves killed their masters and burned plantations. This went on for almost a month. Then, as the slaves paused to decide their next move, two things happened. The desperate French planters asked the British for help. The British, hoping to take over the island, agreed. But a new slave leader, Toussaint L'Ouverture, emerged. He led the slaves to victory over the British. By 1800 the slave revolt had succeeded. In 1801 French San Domingo was renamed Haiti. The French tried to invade it. They captured L'Ouverture and he died in prison in 1803. But Haiti was not recaptured for long. The people drove the French out and declared themselves an independent country in 1804.

Source C

A print, made at the time, showing the San Domingo uprising. Stories about the uprising spread around the world, causing slave owners to worry even more about slave rebellions.

Resistance on the *Amistad*

In April 1839 Cinque, the son of a West African chief of the Mendi people, was sold in Cuba. He and fifty other slaves were sold to two Spaniards for their South American plantation. The Spaniards hired a ship, the *Amistad*, to take the slaves there. That night, the slaves rose up, stole the sailors' weapons and took over the ship. The captain and the cook were killed, but the rest of the crew were set adrift in a small boat. The slaves, with Cinque in charge, told the Spaniards ● sail the ship back to Africa.

Instead, the Spanish sailed north and west, arriving off Long Island in August. The US Navy took the ship to New Haven, Connecticut. Here, except for three little girls, the slaves were arrested for killing the captain of the *Amistad*.

Source D

Cinque, painted in New Haven in about 1840.

White supporters in New Haven found a black Mendi seaman, James Covey, to talk to the slaves. He helped them campaign to have the slaves released. The newspapers were full of the story and there was a lot of argument over the case.

The first trial

The first trial lasted all winter. The jury said the slaves were innocent. But their opponents appealed, and demanded that the case go to the Supreme Court, the most important court in the United States.

The second trial

John Quincy Adams, a lawyer who had been President of the United States, spoke up for the slaves in the Supreme Court. He was seventy-three, retired and almost blind, but his arguments were so powerful that the Supreme Court agreed that the slaves should be freed and taken back to West Africa. In 1841 they went, taking with them two Christian missionaries who set up the first anti-slavery mission in Africa.

Fugitive slave laws

Although some states in the North did not allow slavery, this did not mean they were safe places for slaves who fled there from the South. From 1793 onwards, fugitive slave laws said it was wrong for people in free states to hide or help runaway slaves. If people in free states found out that a black person was a runaway, they had to return that person to his or her owner. If they did not, they could be imprisoned. So the law treated slaves as property even in places where slavery did not exist.

The Dred Scott case

Resistance on the *Amistad* had begun with violence, but victory was won in court. More and more black people turned to the courts for justice, but they did not always get it. The verdict of one of the most famous court cases of the time struck a terrible blow against the rights of black people.

Dred Scott, his wife Harriet and daughters Eliza and Lizzie were born in Virginia. They had moved around with their master, and had spent four years living in free states. Scott had saved to buy the family's freedom, but his owner refused to accept the payment. So, in 1847, Scott used the $300 he had saved to sue for freedom. He argued that living in states that did not accept slavery had made him free. A court in the town of St Louis agreed. It was overruled by the state court, which said Scott and his family were still slaves. Their master promptly sold them. Scott took the case to the Supreme Court.

In 1857 the Supreme Court turned down Scott's appeal. It said: *Negroes are inferior beings who have no rights which the white man is bound to respect*. It also said blacks could not be US citizens, because the Declaration of Independence and the Constitution were never meant to apply to them. Also, it was illegal to take away *human articles of merchandise* (slaves) from their owners, even in free states. So Scott and his family were still slaves. They were later freed, and lived in St Louis, where Scott worked in a hotel.

The case was important. If Scott had won, black people would have had their rights recognised. Slave owners would have worried about taking slaves into free states. But Scott lost. Worse than that, issues that had been confused before the case had now been clearly set out by the most important court in the USA. Black people had no rights. They could not be taken from their owners. They were just property.

Source E

Things to do

1 a What was the difference between passive resistance and active resistance?

b Why might a slave choose to resist passively, not actively?

c Why might a slave choose to resist actively, not passively?

2 In what ways did the *Amistad* case:

a help black people gain rights?

b make it harder for black people to gain rights?

Black people who ran away to free states lived in danger of recapture. Many black people joined a nearby Native American Indian tribe instead. Most tribes happily accepted black people and treated them as equals.

Slaves tried to escape all the time. They might make it on their own, but many did not, because they were forced to give up by hunger or were found out.

The 'underground railroad'

Many slaves who escaped did so with the help of the 'underground railroad'. This was a secret organisation of black and white people who took escaping slaves from one safe house (called a 'station') to another, all the way to freedom in the North. The people who took the slaves from one station to another were called 'conductors'. The conductors and people who ran stations took big risks, especially black people in slave states. Because it was a secret organisation, there is not much written evidence about the underground railroad. We know that about 3200 people worked on it, and that from 1830 to 1860 about 75,000 slaves escaped on it. Some were recaptured, but many stayed free.

HARRIET TUBMAN: ONE 'CONDUCTOR'

Harriet Tubman was a runaway slave who worked on the underground railroad. She made about twenty trips, taking huge risks to help other slaves escape. Tubman was said to threaten to shoot any 'passengers' who spoke of tiredness or turning back. She knew it was important to keep going. She took her passengers all the way to Canada, not trusting the free states. In the North during the American Civil War she worked for the northern army as a spy, scout and nurse. After the war she campaigned for black rights and women's rights. She died in 1913.

John Jones, painted when he was a rich and respected Chicago businessman. He had a lot to lose if his association with the underground railroad was found out.

JOHN JONES: ONE 'STATION'

John Jones was a free black man, born in 1816 in North Carolina. He and his wife moved to Chicago, Illinois, in 1845, with just $3.50. Jones worked as a tailor and grew steadily richer and more respected by black and white people alike. Jones and his wife also fought slavery. Their home was a station on the underground railroad.

Jones and his wife fought openly against the various 'black laws' in Illinois, which stopped black people voting or being witnesses in court. In January 1865 Illinois got rid of its black laws and abolished slavery.

Jones became involved in politics and was elected to several government jobs. He battled to open all Chicago schools to black and white pupils. This was finally accepted in 1874, five years before Jones died.

Source A

People did escape without the help of the underground railroad. Educated slaves who planned their escape and had the help of friends were most likely to stay free. Uneducated slaves with no help and no plan beyond escape were often recaptured.

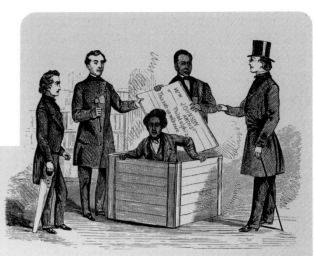

A drawing from the time showing Henry Brown's release from his box.

HENRY BROWN

One famous slave escape story is that of Henry 'Box' Brown. Brown had been sold to the owner of a tobacco factory in Richmond. His new master refused to buy Brown's wife. So Brown thought up a plan for escape.

I decided to shut myself up in a box and get myself sent to a free state as dry goods. My friend Dr Smith agreed to help me. We found a storekeeper willing to help. He wrote to a friend in Philadelphia, who agreed to have the parcel addressed to him. I had a box made 1.1m long, 75cm high and 60cm wide. I got permission to be away from work for a few days, not to be missed at once. I made a breathing hole in the part of the box where my face would be, and took with me a small amount of water. On the morning of 29 March 1849, I was nailed into the box by my friends and taken to the Express Office to be posted.

The carrier put the box on its end, despite the sign that said, 'This side up with care.' So I began the journey head down. Luckily the box tumbled over in the journey to the steamboat. But I was put on the steamboat head downwards again. I was left like this for an hour and a half. I felt my eyes ready to burst from my sockets. The veins on my face swelled hugely. But I made no noise, determined to be free or die. Then my box was turned up for a passenger to sit on.

At Washington I was taken by wagon to the depot. Here I was tossed from the wagon, despite protests by the driver that if the label said 'with care' something might break. As I fell my neck gave a crack, and I was knocked out. I awoke as I was loaded onto a wagon, head down again. I was soon turned over to make room for more boxes. I was left right side up until we reached Philadelphia. We arrived at the depot at 3 a.m. At 6 a.m. my box was collected and carried to the right address. A number of people came round the box, but seemed unwilling to open it. Then one of them rapped on the box and asked, 'Is all right within?' to which I replied, 'All right.' They broke open the box and I was free.

Things to do

1 a Why do you think the 'underground railroad' was given its name?

 b Why do you think slaves needed it?

2 Give some advice to slaves thinking of escaping. What should they take? What should they do? What should they not do?

3 You are a journalist on a northern newspaper written by, and for, black people. Tell the story of Henry Brown in 150 words.

3.6 WHAT WAS IT LIKE TO BE A SLAVE?

In the 1930s, the US government sent people to talk to ex-slaves about their experiences of slavery before 1865. Here are just a few stories of slavery in North Carolina.

HENRY TRENTHAM

*I was born near Camden, on Dr Trentham's plantation. My family lived there too. It was an awfully big plantation, with about 400 slaves. The slave houses looked like a small town. There was a mill for the corn, a **cotton gin**, shoe shops, **tanning yards** and lots of cloth-weaving looms. Master had four overseers. They drove us from sun-up to sunset. Women had to keep up with the men. Most slaves cooked at their houses. We got weekly rations – pretty good, like what you'd have now.*

*We got a week holiday over Christmas, and got our shoes for the year. On the Fourth of July there'd be a big dinner, barbecue and cake. There was a church, where the preacher told us to do as we were told. We weren't allowed books, so I can't read or write. There was a jail for punishment. I saw slaves whipped by the **overseers**, but mostly if slaves didn't suit Master, he sold them on. Missus didn't like him to beat them much.*

MATTIE CURTIS

I was born on the Hayes plantation, but me and my family were sold to a speculator called Bubb, who sold us up by the Franklin and Granville border. We was sold to a preacher named Whitfield. For all he was a preacher he hardly fed or clothed his 20 slaves, and he whipped them bad. He'd take off your clothes, tie you to a barrel in his sitting room and beat the blood out of you. My job was to mind the slaves' children while they were out in the tobacco fields.

Whitfield never paid for us, so we got sold on to a Missus Long in Franklin County. She was a devil. I was about fifteen now and had to work in her tobacco factory. We stemmed it, rolled it and packed it for selling. The Civil War started while we was with her. She sold us on during the war to Moses Mordicia, near Raleigh. He was just as bad as her, if not worse.

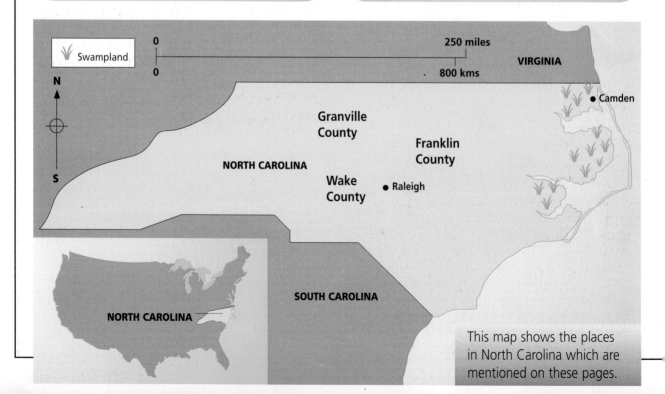

This map shows the places in North Carolina which are mentioned on these pages.

Five generations of slaves on a South Carolina plantation.

RIA SORRELL

I was born on the Sorrell plantation, near Leesville, Wake County. There were about 25 slaves on the place. The Master wouldn't sell us, and he didn't believe in whipping. His wife was a devil, though, she loved to whip us when the Master was away, gone to town. She used to want to not feed us, but he used to bring us food, said people couldn't work without eating. He'd eat with us, sometimes.

Master Sorrell gave us good houses, two rooms fixed right and good beds with enough covers. We had a patch of ground to grow things on too. We worked sun-up till sunset, but we had no overseers. Master didn't believe in them. He told the oldest slaves, father was one, what he wanted doing, and they told us and we done it.

We got holidays Christmas, Sundays and one day a month. Mind, he wouldn't allow no reading nor writing. But he let us go to church.

PATSY MITCHNER

I was born in Raleigh. My Master was Alex Gorman, the newspaper man. The slaves turned the wheels and the white men done the printing – we was not let read or write. They sold my mother, sister and brother to a slave speculator who shipped them down to Mississippi. Our clothes and sleeping places were bad. In slavery time the food was real bad, meat all fat and just cornbread. No good food for the nigger at Master's. I never saw a slave sold in chains or a jail. I never saw a whipping – whippings was in the back shed.

Things to do

1 Write a short radio script about slavery in North Carolina. Include:
  - size of the plantations
  - food and homes
  - work and names
  - whipping and punishments.

2 a What was the one thing no one was allowed to do?
  b Why do you think this was?

A divided nation

Slavery set slave and free states in the Union (the United States) against each other. Any division of the states had always been seen as a problem (see page 20). But the southern states grew more and more angry with northerners who tried to end slavery, refused to return escaped slaves and helped slaves to run away. Northerners were tired of southerners refusing to end slavery.

In 1858 Abraham Lincoln, a representative for Illinois, said: *A house divided against itself cannot stand. This government cannot always be half-slave and half-free.* He said the Union would survive, but the states must no longer be divided. He meant the slave states had to give up slavery. Lincoln wanted freedom, but not equality, for black people. He said: *I am not in favour of bringing about the social and political equality of white and black races.*

Separate nations?

In July 1859 an anti-slavery campaigner, John Brown, tried to start an armed slave rebellion. He was caught and executed, along with his followers, black and white. The South felt it was at risk of being invaded and forced to abolish slavery. Then, in November 1860, Lincoln was elected President. Six weeks after his election South Carolina left the Union. The states of Mississippi, Florida, Alabama, Georgia, Louisiana and Texas followed. In February 1861 they set up the **Confederate States of America**. The split Lincoln had not expected had happened after all. He had misjudged the strength of feeling in the South about the right of southern states to choose for themselves. He scrabbled to hold the Union together. But it was too late. How many more states would join the Confederates?

Source A

The Governor of Texas, Sam Houston, was thrown out of office when he tried to stop Texas leaving the Union. He made the following speech.

Let me tell you what is coming. Your fathers, your husbands, your sons and brothers will be herded at the point of a bayonet. You may, after sacrificing countless millions of dollars and hundreds of thousands of lives, just possibly win southern independence. But I doubt it. The North is determined to preserve the Union.

The division of the United States.

■	The Confederate states
▨	The Union states

UPPER CANADA

UNITED STATES

MEXICO

Gulf of Mexico

Atlantic Ocean

No Union left?

We now know that not all states in the South joined the Confederates. But at the time there was no way of knowing how many would join. Lincoln was worried that so many would join that the North would be seriously outnumbered. A lawyer summed up feelings when he said: *All the signs are that this infection [joining the Confederacy] is making steady progress across the Union, week by week.*

Fighting for freedom?

In April 1861 war broke out. Black people wanted to fight. The Union government feared this would push more states to join the Confederates. It said slaves who ran away to join the Union army had to be sent back to their masters. Many commanders refused to do this. They called the runaway slaves contraband (smuggled property) and let them work for the army. As late as August 1862 Lincoln was still hoping to salvage peace, saying: *My chief aim is to keep the Union together. If I could save the Union without freeing any slave, I would do it. If I could save it by freeing all slaves, I would do it. If I could save it by freeing some and leaving others alone, I would do that.*

Finally the government gave in. The **Emancipation Proclamation** of January 1863 freed slaves in 'rebel' (Confederate) states and let black men join the army. But they were not treated equally. Most were organised into black units led by white officers. They were paid less: $7 a month when whites got $13. In Massachusetts the all-black 54th Regiment served for a year without pay rather than accept a lower wage.

The war ends

The war, which was the bloodiest that America has ever been involved in, lasted until March 1865. The northern Unionist army won. Five days after the war ended, President Lincoln was assassinated.

A JOB FOR THE NEW CABINET MAKER.

A cartoon published at the time, showing Lincoln trying to paste the Union together.

Source C

Frederick Douglass, a black anti-slavery campaigner, welcomed the splitting of the United States and urged black people to become involved in the war.

Every consideration of justice, humanity and sound policy confirms the wisdom of calling on black men to take up arms in defence of their country. We are ready.

Things to do

1 a Which were the two sides in the Civil War?
  b How were their views on slavery different?

2 Why did the Union not allow black people to join their army at first?

3 'Lincoln was a great supporter of black rights.' Use the information on these pages to explain why you agree or disagree with this statement.

The Civil War and the Emancipation Proclamation had different effects on black people.

Soldiers

Many black men who had been slaves in the South ran away from their masters to join the Union army (the 'Yankees').

ROBERT HOUSTON'S WARTIME TRAVELS

After the war, Robert Houston told a court of his wartime experiences:

After the Yankees took Memphis we slaves were told by the Confederate Army to make defences, but we ran and hid in the woods. We made our way to the Mississippi River and got taken on by the Union Marine Fleet at $60 a month for two months. Just before the time was up I got smallpox, so was put off on an island. I lived there for several months, cutting and selling wood. Then a Federal Steamboat came and took all the men off the Island and swore us into the Union army. They also bought my wood and gave me a receipt to be paid. I joined up willingly and have always done all I could to support the Union cause and have never helped the rebels, as far as I know. But when I was sworn up they said I would have to wait till the end of the war to be paid and now the receipt is lost.

THE BATTLE OF PORT HUDSON

A white commanding officer tells of the bravery of his black troops at the battle of Port Hudson, Louisiana:

My company was largely contrabands, so when it came to it I had worries about their bravery. Now I have none. They obeyed the order to advance the moment it was given, and advanced under the most murderous fire as if marching on parade. When forced to retreat they held together and split into groups to skirmish. We alone held our position from 6 a.m. until noon. At 2 p.m. we were ordered to make two charges against the enemy guns. Their fire would have confused and disorganised any troops. Yet these men did not swerve, or show any cowardice. I have been in several battles, but never with soldiers of such coolness and daring. The sneers of many when they joined have turned to praise.

The battle at Port Hudson, 27 May 1863.

Source A

Families

The Union army did not really want whole families. Some men left their families behind, sometimes with disastrous consequences. Other families fled together, setting up home in contraband camps – makeshift homes set up near the army camps. This did not always work, either.

MARTHA GLOVER

30 December 1863

My Dear Husband,
I have received your kind letter, and was pleased to hear from you. It seems a long time since you left. I have had nothing but trouble since. I told you how it would be if you went. They beat and insult me and will not look after me and our children. You ought never to have left me in the fix I am in, with all these helpless little children to take care of. The children talk about you all the time. I do not know what will become of me, or them. Oh I wish you had stayed with me, and not gone till I could go with you, I do nothing but grieve for you all the time. Do not ask me to beg married men to go. I've seen too much trouble to get into any more.
Farewell dear husband, from your wife, Martha

Six weeks later Martha was separated from most of her children. She and her three youngest were taken to Kentucky to be sold.

Things to do

Use the sources on this page to answer the following questions. Give examples.

1 What were the advantages and disadvantages of joining the army for black soldiers?

2 When black slaves ran away to join the Yankees, was it better for their families to go with them or to stay behind?

Source B

Contraband families, freed as the Union army moved south.

JOSEPH MILLER'S FAMILY

My wife and children came with me when I joined up in October 1864. My master had said if I enlisted he would not look after them. I had four children, aged ten, nine, seven and four. I was shown a tent in the Camp, where my family could stay. They had permission to use it. On 22 November, in the evening, my wife was told they had to leave by morning. My son had been sick and they had no place to go. At about eight in the morning, an armed guard ordered my family out of the Camp, in weather so cold I was sure my son would die if taken out. I told the guard I was a US soldier and that it would be the death of my son to go. There was a wagon ready. The guard said they had to get in it, or he would shoot them. They went and were taken to Nicholasville, some six miles from the Camp. When I found them that evening they were cold and had not been fed all day. My boy was dead. I had to leave them and go back to Camp. The next night I went back. I dug a grave myself and buried my own child.

The Civil War was over. The South had lost. Emancipation (freedom from slavery) soon followed. In 1865 the Thirteenth Amendment abolished slavery. A **Freedmen's Bureau** was set up to start schools and help black people find work. Reconstruction (establishing freedom in the South) began in 1867, backed by the army. The Fourteenth Amendment (1866) made black people full US citizens – not three fifths of a person. The Fifteenth Amendment (1870) gave black men equal voting rights with white men. So did black people live freely and equally with white people?

Source A

Langston Hughes, a black poet and historian, summed up the atmosphere in the South after the war.

'The Yankees freed you, now let the Yankees feed you,' was the attitude of most former Confederates after the war. The South was a shambles. Its major cities were gutted, its farms neglected, its crops ungathered, its banks closed. About a third of its men had been killed or wounded in the war.

Steps forward

Freedom

For the first time, freed slaves could marry and have children without fearing that their family would be split up. They could work, move around and worship God as they wanted. Black churches became more than just a place to worship. They were meeting places, and often had schools attached to them. Black men could also vote, stand for election, sit on juries and become judges. Black men represented southern states in Congress.

Schools

The Freedmen's Bureau set up over 4000 free schools, which took in over 250,000 black students. These schools included primary schools and colleges. When the Bureau shut down in 1870, 21 per cent of freed slaves were able to read and write.

Land

It was suggested that freed slaves should get '40 acres and a mule' to support themselves. This came to nothing. Instead, **sharecropping** was introduced. Free blacks worked the land for a share of the crop they grew. Some black sharecroppers ended up working for their old masters, but as free people.

Hiram Revels, being sworn in as Senator for Mississippi in 1870. Black people were elected to serve for the southern states making local laws, as well as in Congress. So they could try to improve things for black people on a local level.

Source B

Steps back

Freedom

Black people in the South found a difference between their legal rights and what they were allowed to do. They had the right to vote, but were threatened or physically stopped from voting. In some places riots broke out over black voting, and many black people were killed. It was no good having rights which were not enforced.

Schools and land

Many southern schools closed because whites would not sell them supplies. Some schools were burned down and students beaten up. A seventeen-year-old black teacher was murdered for starting a school in Tennessee.

Sharecroppers had to buy tools and supplies from planters' shops. The money to pay for this came out of their 'share'. Many found that they spent more than their share could cover each year, so they fell into debt.

'Jim Crow' laws

In 1877 the new President took the army out of the South, and life became harder for black people there. Southern states passed 'Jim Crow' laws to 'put blacks in their place' by **segregation**. The idea of segregation was for black people to live separate lives. They had separate places on buses, in theatres and in churches. They had separate schools. Even public toilets and water fountains were labelled for use by 'whites' or 'coloureds'. There was still no real equality, either. Black people got the worst of the deal. Many shops and restaurants refused to serve black customers at all. Some black churches said people might be better off moving north or west. Many went.

'Ship 'em out'

Some people, both black and white, felt the solution to tensions between black and white people was for black people to go back to Africa. In about 1817 the American Colonisation Society bought land in Africa and created a country called Liberia. The first black colonists went to Liberia in 1822. But the colony was criticised by both black and white people, and never really got off the ground. Even so, it was suggested as a solution again in the 1860s. But most black people chose to move within America.

Things to do

1 How did things change in the South for black people after 1865?

2 Do you think emancipation was a success or failure? Make a list of points to support each side.

Source C

The Ku Klux Klan was an extreme group of whites that sprang up in 1865. Dressed in white robes and hoods, they terrorised black people right across the southern states. Despite the fact that they killed many black people, it was hard to catch or prosecute them, because policemen and judges were Klan members, too. So they got away with murder.

This photograph shows one of the Klan ceremonies to choose new members.

What happened to the slaves in North Carolina after the war? Did they think freedom had improved their lives? This is what they said.

PATSY MITCHNER

When I was about twelve it was the war. The southern cavalry came through and stole all they could. Everyone left the Gormans so I went to an aunt at Rolesville, then we all came to Raleigh. I'll tell you, before two years had passed after the surrender two out of every three slaves wished they was back with their masters.

Slavery was better for us than things now, well, some of us. Had no responsibility, just work, eat, sleep. Slaves prayed for freedom, got it and didn't know what to do with it. Slavery was a bad thing. But the freedom they got, with nothing to live on, that was bad, too. Like two snakes. Both bit the nigger, and both was bad. Lots of masters took them back. Some white folks were hard, some looked after their slaves. I bin working for white folks, washing and cooking, ever since freedom came.

MATTIE CURTIS

When the Yankees come, they come and freed us. Right after the war, northern preachers came around to marry all that wanted marrying. They married my mammy and pappy and tried to find their fourteen oldest children, who had been sold on. They never did find but three of them.

Some corporation cut the land up, but the slaves ain't got none I heard of. I married Josh Curtis and bought fifteen acres from the land corporation. I cut the trees and sold the wood and cleared and ploughed the land and planted it. Josh helped build the house, and worked on the land some. I finally paid for the land, and had nineteen children. Josh died, and fifteen of the children, though they lived to be near grown. I kept on going. I'll never forget my first bale of cotton. I was some proud of that bale. I took it to Raleigh. The white folk hated the nigger then, specially if they was making something, so I didn't ask where the market was. I couldn't find it, so I went home. I went back next day, asked a policeman. He took me there and I sold my bale.

Source A

HENRY TRENTHAM

After the War, I married Ella Davis. We stayed in near Camden. We had twelve children, six boys and six girls. I think slavery was pretty rough, and I'm glad it's all over.

Not all freed slaves could become sharecroppers. Many had to take on work as field hands. Some of them ended up working for their old owners.

This painting of a free family was made in 1881. It shows a preacher visiting a black family. Freedom meant families could worship as they wanted. They could also start a family knowing that family members would not be sold off at any time.

Source C

Not everyone co-operated with the interviewers in 1930. Thomas Hall explains why he would not co-operate:

When I think of slavery, it makes me mad. I do not believe in giving you my story, because with all the promises that have been made, the Negro is still in a bad way in the US, no matter what part he lives in, it's all the same. You are going around to get a story of the slavery and persecutions of the Negroes before the Civil War, and the economic conditions concerning them since that war. You should have known, before this late date, about all that. No matter where you are from I don't want you to write my story, because the white folks have been, are now and will always be against the Negro.

RIA SORRELL

Yes, I remember the Yankees. Our soldiers was running away from them and taking foods and animals and even the quilts off the beds as they went. Then the Yankees came and took what was left. That was a time. There wasn't much left when they was both through! When they told us we were free we stayed with our Master. When the crop was in the Master gave us part of all we made. We got an allowance of meat and crackers from the Yankees, we had to go to Raleigh to fetch it.

After Master died we moved to the Paige place, eleven miles north of Raleigh. I was married by then, to Buck Sorrell. We had six children, all but one died. We been farming with the white folks ever since, till we got so we couldn't work. Slavery was a bad thing, cause some white folk didn't treat their niggers right.

Things to do

Use the information on these pages to make a chart listing the good and bad effects of emancipation. By each effect say whose evidence you have used to find this.

On paper, black people were US citizens, with equal rights, by 1880. In practice they faced racial prejudice, segregation and violence. These things were more extreme in the South, but even in the North and West black people went to their own schools, and shopped, ate and lived in their own parts of town. They were less likely to live in pleasant areas, go to good schools or get a job. They were 'last hired, first fired'. Even in New York, a city said to welcome black people, a suburb set up in 1886 openly excluded black people, Jews and Catholics.

Source A

George Washington Carver teaching chemistry at the Tuskegee Institute. This college for black students was set up by an escaped black slave, Booker T. Washington.

Challenging segregation

In 1898 Homer Plessy challenged the Louisiana railway company's right to make him sit in a 'black' railway carriage. His lawyer argued, *our Constitution is colour blind.* The Supreme Court was not. It said segregation was legal as long as each race had 'equal' provision, which black people never had. After this, the South increased levels of segregation.

Education

Black people worked hard to improve their situation. Their biggest weapon in the fight for equality was a good education. This was hard to get. Teachers in black schools earned less and black schools were less well equipped. Even so, black people learned, passed exams and became doctors, lawyers and teachers. They all helped fight the idea that black people were unintelligent.

Source B

In 1913, Woodrow Wilson, the first southern President of the USA since the Civil War, set up segregation in government offices, saying:

Slavery did more for the Negro in 250 years than African freedom has done since the building of the pyramids. Segregation is not humiliating, but a benefit, and ought to be so regarded by you.

Organise!

Churches were the first black organisations – an important force in getting black people to act. From 1900, other movements were set up to organise protests and demands for action:

Movement	Aims	Set up
National Negro Business League	To help black businesses	1900
Niagara Movement	To fight for black rights to the vote and equality	1905
National Association for the Advancement of Colored People (NAACP)	To fight for black rights	1909
National Urban League	To help black people who move to the cities to find homes and jobs and to register for government help	1911

These black officers led black units in France during the First World War. They are wearing medals given to them by the French for bravery.

The First World War

The First World War broke out in Europe in 1914. The Allies (Britain and France) asked the USA to help them fight Germany. The USA would not fight, but helped by lending money and selling equipment to the Allies. America finally joined the war in 1917. Black people, including members of the NAACP, joined the army and campaigned for equality in the armed forces.

Black contributions to the war

The government promised to train black officers if 200 black college students joined the army; 15,000 applied. In October 1917 the first group of 639 black officers qualified. But black officers had to command black units, and black people could not join white units. Black men could not join the Marines or become officers in the navy.

Black people contributed to the war in other ways. Garret A. Morgan, a black scientist, invented the gas mask. Blacks moved north to work in factories making war goods. But wherever they moved, violence somehow occurred, because they were competing with white people for this work.

After the war

Tensions between poor whites and blacks increased after the war. They were in even greater competition for work and places to live. Employers did nothing to calm the tensions – it was better for them if the poor whites were fighting blacks than joining with them to oppose the bosses. The Ku Klux Klan started up again in the South, and **lynchings** became common. But violence did not only happen in the South. In 1919, there were more than twenty-five major race riots all over the country.

Things to do

1 What was segregation?

2 In what ways were black people in the North not treated equally?

3 a Why did Homer Plessy take his case to the Supreme Court?
  b How did the result make things worse for black people?

4 How would Woodrow Wilson (Source B) explain why he felt slavery and segregation were good for black people?

5 Make a poster telling black people to fight for an education. Make it clear why this is important.

6 How did black people help in the First World War?

7 How did things get worse for black people after the war?

The years before and after the First World War were a time of contradictions. Black people were making real progress, but they were also being treated in a way that made equality seem as far away as ever.

BOOKER T. WASHINGTON

Booker T. Washington was an escaped slave who set up the Tuskegee Institute in 1881. It was true that Tuskegee gave black people a chance of an education. But it was a segregated college. It also stressed 'practical' skills – which annoyed many black people. Washington said, *there is as much dignity in tilling a field as in writing a poem.* He felt whites needed time to accept black equality. He reassured them about segregation: *in all things social we can be as separate as fingers, yet work as one hand.* His critics complained: *He is the leader not of one race but of two – a compromiser between the South, the North and the Negro.*

W.E.B. DU BOIS

William Du Bois set up the National Negro Business League in 1900. He was against the idea of educating black people mostly in practical skills. He said of Booker T. Washington, *while he – or the South, or the Nation – opposes the higher training of our brighter minds, we must oppose them.* He felt that under-educating black people just reinforced the white idea that black people were not as clever as whites.

Du Bois had been well educated, in the USA and abroad, and became head of history and economics at Atlanta University. He headed the Niagara Movement, whose aims were:

- to work against corruption in politics
- to organise 'intelligent and honest Negroes' to fight for civil rights and the right to work and worship
- to set up newspapers and other groups to give people a say.

Du Bois was one of the people who set up the NAACP, and he edited its newspaper, *Crisis*, from 1909 to 1932.

Source A

As the lynchings and segregation went on, a Niagara Movement meeting in 1906 announced:

In the past year the work of the Negro-hater has flourished. Step by step defenders of the rights of American citizens have retreated. We want the right to vote and we want it now. We want segregation to cease. We want to mix freely with whoever we want. We want the laws of this country enforced against the rich, as well as the poor, white as well as black. We want our children educated. They have a right to know, to think, to aspire.

Source B

Girls at Tuskegee learning how to be maids.

Duke Ellington and his band performing at the Cotton Club, Harlem.

Harlem

The Harlem area of New York was famous in the 1920s and 1930s as a centre of black culture. Black people composed and performed serious music, musicals and jazz, and wrote novels and poetry. Real black actors – not white people in black make-up – played black people. White people came to listen to Duke Ellington play music and to hear Ella Fitzgerald sing. They admitted, maybe for the first time, that black people could do things as well as and often better than whites. Harlem was more than a cultural centre. Black people could feel at home and in charge in Harlem, not on the outside and in danger. Loften Mitchell, who grew up there in the 1930s, said: *It was distinct from the rest of the city, like a small town. Newcomers, relatives and strangers, were welcomed and helped to find a home and a job. Everyone knew everyone else. A kid was misbehaving he was punished by those who saw him, then when he got home. You might be cooking one thing when a neighbour would drop in with something else and so on until a family meal turned into a party.*

ELTON FAX

Elton Fax moved to Harlem from Baltimore in the 1930s:

I saw Harlem first in the 1930s. It wasn't just the big things either. Let me tell you one of the little things that meant so much. Lacy, a big black policeman, was directing traffic. White folks had to stop and go at his bidding. Where I came from no black person was in charge that way. He'd pull over a car full of white folks and stroll over. And he'd say, 'As big and black as I am, you mean to tell me you didn't see my hand in the air?' And he'd book them. It might seem unimportant, but it was impressive.

Outside Harlem

Carter Woodson, a black historian, set up Negro History Week (now Black History Week) in 1926. Woodson went to the only inter-racial college in the USA, Berea College, Kentucky. He set up the Association for the Study of Negro Life and History in 1915 and published the *Journal of Negro History*.

There were black professors, scientists and inventors. Black doctors included Dr Hale Williams, the first doctor to operate successfully on the human heart.

Things to do

1 a How did black people in Harlem make progress towards equality in the 1920s?

  b How much progress did black people make outside Harlem?

2 Why did Booker T. Washington think that his remark about hands and fingers would reassure white people?

3 a Source A on page 40 and Source B on page 42 show the Tuskegee Institute. Which shows the 'practical skills' that some black people objected to?

  b Why did they object?

5.3 BAD TIMES: THE DEPRESSION

What was the Depression?

In the 1920s many people in the USA were making money. Businesses were doing well. People bought shares in companies, which meant they got a share of the profits. It was easy to make money and find work. More black people did well, too. More black people became doctors, teachers, politicians and lawyers. There were still a lot of poor people, black and white, but people were hopeful about ending poverty altogether as employment rose. But in 1929 there was a sudden change. Businesses started to do less well. People panicked and sold their shares all at once. Because of this, many people, businesses, even banks lost all their money. Many people lost their jobs, and even their homes.

The situation was made worse because the farmland of the Midwest of the USA was hit by a terrible drought. The soil dried out and became useless for farming. Farmers lost all their money and there was less food. Huge numbers of people, black and white, became **migrants**, moving around the country looking for work. But there were far more people than jobs. Historians have estimated that up to 50 million migrants were out of work in the 1930s.

How were black people affected?

Before the Depression there were many poorly paid jobs that only black people would do – 'Negro jobs' like cleaning rubbish from the streets. When the Depression hit, Whites were desperate for any work. Black people were sacked. 'Negro jobs' were given to white people.

What did the government do to help?

At first, the government, led by President Hoover, did not help. It said people should help themselves. However, in 1932 President Roosevelt began to help. His government set up agencies to feed and house people and to help them find work.

Good and bad effects

There were more black people in this government than ever before. Help and training were given to both Blacks and Whites. But many people were still suffering, and this made Whites more likely to hit out at Blacks. Race riots broke out in various parts of the country. Lynchings in the South were so common that the sight of black people hanging from trees was almost an everyday one.

Source A

FATHER DIVINE

Father Divine was a black church leader who told his followers not to take government help. Instead, he set up shops selling cheap food and coal to poor people, both black and white. People worked for and looked after each other. Father Divine also set up restaurants that fed people cheaply or for free.

One of Father Divine's restaurants.

Town or country?

Were black people better off farming, or working in cities? There had been a stream of black people moving to the northern cities ever since emancipation. They hoped to find work and greater equality than in the South. Different people had different experiences. It depended on who you were and where you were.

JANE MAXWELL

Jane was born in the South in 1916 and began doing housework in 1928. She earned $1.50 a week. She married in 1932 and had a son. Her husband left a month after the baby was born. Jane worked, while her mother looked after the baby. The whole family was often ill. She was told that a friend could find her work in New York. He took her and seven other black women there. Jane found work as a live-in cleaner for $7 a week and sent for her family to join her. When interviewed in 1940 she was out of work, but getting by on government relief of $28 for her and her mother. Their rent was $22, but she said she was sure they were better off in New York, where there was more chance of finding work.

Source B

Black farmers talking about the problems of farming during the Depression.

If it wasn't grubs eating the cotton plants it was the drought. If it wasn't the drought it was the rains. What kills us is we just can't make it here. They pay us nothing for what we give them and then they charge us double price when they sell it back to us.

Source C

A black sharecropper in Mississippi was interviewed in 1942 about the Depression. He warned his interviewer that it was not as simple as the North being liberal and the South being racist.

There was a lot of hate in the 1930s. There were race riots in the northern cities. We had hate here too, lynchings. I'm not saying the white and black people loved each other then, or now either. But we went through a lot together. We were all suffering, black and white. We helped each other out. We weren't equal, no question. But we had white friends, white neighbours who'd talk to you, send over food, get you to a doctor. I tried Chicago. It was worse up there. No one would even say hello. They got violent up there, invaded our streets, killed our people. I came back to Mississippi.

Things to do

Write an outline for a debate between Jane Maxwell and the sharecropper (Source C) about whether it was better to live through the Depression in the countryside or in a city.

Source D

Black migrant families in the 1920s.

The Depression hit black people hard. It also raised the level of resentment that white people, especially poor white people, felt towards blacks. It was hard to believe that equality was possible. Black people began to think that maybe separation – choosing to live apart from white people in totally black communities – was the best option.

Separation: not a new idea

The idea of separation had been around for almost as long as there had been free blacks in the USA. In 1820 a few black people went to Liberia, in Africa (see page 37), to set up a black nation of their own. But most people felt that the USA was their homeland. Those who left the South moved north and west. But they found that they did not have equal rights there, either. The idea of going to Liberia was raised from time to time, but it was never very successful.

Black pride

By the 1920s, many people felt that existing black organisations were getting nowhere in the fight for black rights. Marcus Garvey's Universal Negro Improvement Association (UNIA) seemed more attractive. Garvey's message was that black people should not try to fit in with white society. If they did, they would always see themselves as second-rate. Instead, they should be proud of being black. He said that black people should be separate, and should look on Africa as their homeland. His slogan was 'Back to Africa'.

MARCUS GARVEY

Garvey came to the USA from Jamaica in 1916. He set up UNIA in 1917. Whilst many white people and some black people made fun of his ideas, he had a huge following among ordinary people, who gave about $10,000,000 to his cause – despite the fact that many of them were very poor.

Garvey set up the African Orthodox Church, with black images of God and the holy family. He also founded the Black Star Line to transport black people to Liberia. But the ships were not seaworthy. Garvey was arrested in 1923 for fraud, and in 1927 he was sent back to Jamaica. UNIA fell apart without him. He died in 1940 in London.

Source A

Marcus Garvey.

Source B

Some of the things Marcus Garvey said in his speeches.

Black is beautiful.

Up, you mighty race, you can do what you set out to do!

Europe should be for the Europeans, Asia for the Asiatics and Africa for the Africans – 400,000,000 Negroes demand a place in the sun of the world.

Things to do

Why do you think black people supported Marcus Garvey's ideas?

The Second World War

In 1939 the Second World War broke out. At first Germany was fighting Britain and France, but other countries joined in as the war spread. The USA joined the war in 1941, when the Japanese (on Germany's side) bombed the American fleet. The war gave the US economy a big boost, as factories were kept busy making war goods. The outbreak of war helped solve the problem of unemployment, especially as many men joined, or were made to join, the army.

Treated as equals?

When they saw that the USA was likely to join the war, groups such as the NAACP asked the government to train black soldiers in the same way as whites. They said people should be chosen for their abilities, not their colour. They also asked for an end to the segregation of soldiers, doctors and nurses, who were mostly expected to fight in black units and look after black casualties.

Their requests were ignored. One black soldier was promoted to brigadier-general, but black people still could not join the Marines or the Air Corps. They could join the navy, but not to fight, just to work as cooks or waiters. They were still segregated. Even the blood stored by the Red Cross was segregated.

Slow changes

But things did change. In 1941 the army's officer training school began to teach black people alongside whites. In 1942 the navy and Marines started to train black troops. The air force trained black pilots at Tuskegee. In 1945 black and white soldiers fought together in the same unit for the first time in Germany. Over a million black people joined up. About 6000 of them were officers.

Source C

Black women servicing a train in Pennsylvania in 1940.

Wartime America

Black people poured into northern cities to work in the factories, as they had during the First World War. In some places they worked and lived alongside white people. But housing shortages in many cities caused resentment. Black people were an obvious and easy target. There were race riots in several cities. Even when there was no violence, there was still prejudice and segregation. Things became even worse once the war ended and the troops came back looking for work.

Things to do

1 How were the experiences of black soldiers different in the First and Second World Wars?

2 a Why might this raise the expectations of black people after the war?

  b Did things improve after the war? Explain your answer.

From the time of the Civil War onwards, many black people moved north from the southern states. At times, the numbers increased, especially during the two world wars and the many periods of increasing violence in the South. Chicago was an important destination because the road and rail networks led straight there. We are going to look at black migrations to Chicago from Clarksdale, Mississippi.

What was Clarksdale like?

Clarksdale was a town in Mississippi, planned by John Clark in 1868. It was surrounded by farmland and the main crop was cotton. It had no railway until 1879, and no paved streets until 1913. After the Civil War most of the freed slaves who had worked on the cotton plantations became sharecroppers. There was a steady trickle of migration north, mostly to Chicago. Black people lived on the east side of the railway tracks. White people lived on the west side. Black people crossed the tracks only to go to work for white people.

What was Chicago like?

Chicago was a big city. It needed workers for its growing factories. Most black families lived in the South Side of Chicago. People who moved from the South soon discovered that Chicago had segregation and prejudice, too, even if it was less obvious at first. Black people were expected to stay in the South Side. They were paid lower wages and charged more for rooms. In 1910 the rate for the same set of rooms was $25 a month for white people but $37.50 for blacks. All the same, black people who moved there came back talking about more freedom, more work and better pay.

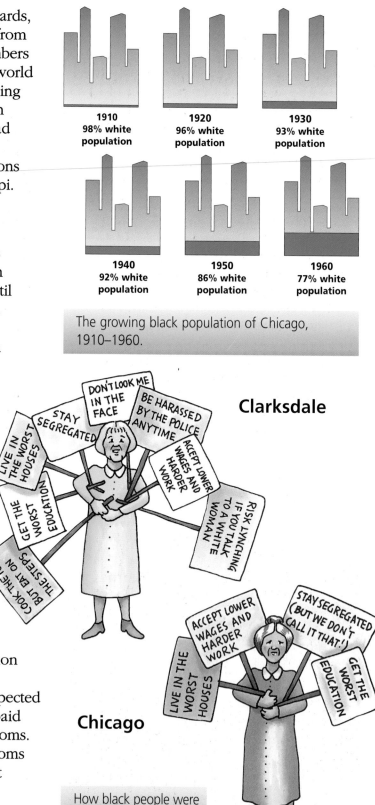

1910
98% white population

1920
96% white population

1930
93% white population

1940
92% white population

1950
86% white population

1960
77% white population

The growing black population of Chicago, 1910–1960.

Clarksdale

DON'T LOOK ME IN THE FACE

BE HARASSED BY THE POLICE ANYTIME

STAY SEGREGATED

LIVE IN THE WORST HOUSES

ACCEPT LOWER WAGES AND HARDER WORK

GET THE WORST EDUCATION

RISK LYNCHING IF YOU TALK TO A WHITE WOMAN

COOK THE FOOD BUT EAT ON THE STEPS

Chicago

ACCEPT LOWER WAGES AND HARDER WORK

STAY SEGREGATED (BUT WE DON'T CALL IT THAT!)

LIVE IN THE WORST HOUSES

GET THE WORST EDUCATION

How black people were expected to live in Clarksdale and Chicago.

RUBY DANIELS

Ruby Daniels was born in 1917. Her father was a sharecropper near Clarksdale. The family scraped by. Ruby drifted around, left by her mother with various relations, mostly close to Clarksdale. In 1934 Ruby married W.D. Daniels. In 1938 they moved to Clarksville on a WPA (Works Progress Administration) work scheme set up during the Depression by the government to find people work.

Ruby worked as a cook for $2.50 a week. If they needed money, she picked cotton on a plantation. In 1940 her aunt, Ceatrice, left her husband and moved to Chicago. In 1941 Ruby's husband joined the army. Ruby, used to a close family but unstable marriages, did not expect him back. She started a relationship with another man, whom she later found out was married. They had two sons, in 1943 and 1944. In 1946 Ruby left her children with relations and moved to Chicago, hoping to start a new life.

A black mother in a Chicago kitchenette in the 1920s.

Source A

Things began well. Ruby and Ceatrice shared a **kitchenette** (small flat) which cost $10 a week. Ruby's cleaning job paid $40.

In 1954 Ceatrice died. Ruby started living with Luther Haynes. They had two sons. Ruby's oldest son looked after the others while Ruby and Luther worked at night. But Luther drifted in and out of jobs, never keeping one for long. They could not afford the rent on their South Side flat. Then the family moved to the West Side. This had become a mainly black, run-down part of Chicago. Ruby and Luther had a daughter. Ruby now had several sons and a baby daughter to support. (Some of the sons were living with relatives.) She had to ask for government aid as well as working. Then Ruby found a flat the family could afford on the South Side. They moved back. Ruby found work cleaning. In 1961 she began to buy a house by making regular payments. But Luther began to buy a car in the same way. They couldn't keep up with both sets of payments. It was the house, not the car, they stopped paying for. They ended up squeezing themselves into a tiny two-roomed flat. They began to argue, and nearly split up. Then Luther found work and Ruby changed jobs. There was more money coming in. In 1962 they got married and moved the family into a newly built block of flats. Here they were settled for a while.

Things to do

1 Why do you think so many black Clarksdale people moved to Chicago?

2 Make a chart to show the ups and downs of Ruby Daniels' life in Chicago. Put starting to buy a home as the high point and moving to the West Side as the lowest.

5.6 PROTEST

In the 1950s and 1960s black people worked together more and more to demand civil rights. Church leaders often led protests. The protests aimed to be non-violent. The images in news reports showed black people not fighting back in the face of white brutality. They were powerful images. More and more white people, especially young white people, joined these protests. In 1960 the Student Non-violent Co-ordinating Committee (SNCC) was set up to organise protesters.

Court cases

Taking cases to court was risky. It relied on the court being fair, rather than biased against black people. If the campaigners won, the decision still had to be enforced. In 1954 judges in the Supreme Court in the *Brown* v. *the Board of Education* case said school segregation was illegal. Southern states urged schools to ignore this. Some schools de-segregated anyway. But in most cases black people had to bring court cases in each state to send their children to 'white' schools. If they won, a few black children, or even just one, had to go to that school to de-segregate it.

Sit-ins and boycotts

Black people deliberately sat in 'white' cafés or restaurants. These protesters were trained to cope with the problems that followed. They were ignored, or cursed, and had food and drink dumped on them. Protesters also rode on segregated buses to de-segregate them.

Campaigners also **boycotted** places that refused them equal rights. They did not use shops or services (such as buses) if they were segregated or did not employ black people. This was one of the first peaceful protest tactics; it was used in the Depression with the slogan 'Don't buy where you can't work'.

Through all their efforts at de-segregation and protest, one of the hardest things for the black people involved was having to be non-violent. If they fought back, their leaders said, they could be removed from the school, the bus or the restaurant. They would have lost. There were no such constraints on the whites who opposed them. Black and white protesters were beaten, threatened and even bombed. Their lives were at risk.

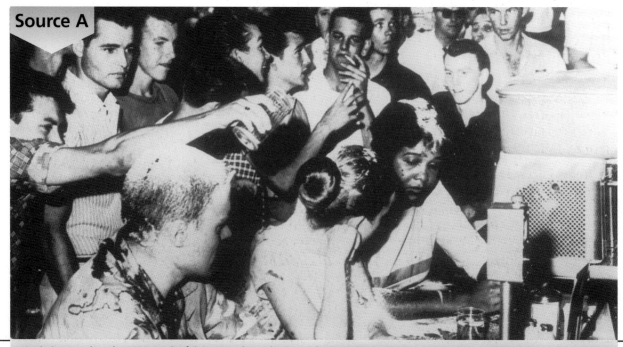

Source A

A sit-in at a lunch counter (café) in Woolworths in Jackson, Mississippi, on 28 May 1963.

The right to vote

Although black people were given the right to vote in 1870, in the South they were still being stopped from doing so in the 1960s.

On 8 June 1964 a government committee interviewed black people about their experiences of trying to vote.

FANNIE LOU HAMER

Fannie Lou Hamer was a sharecropper in Ruleville, Mississippi, who joined the SNCC after going to one of its meetings. She then tried to register to vote. She lost her job because of this. She set up the Mississippi Freedom Democratic Party. By 1970 she was so famous that there was a 'Fanny Lou Hamer Day' holiday in Ruleville.

On 31 August 1962 I went to the county court house to register to vote. I was fired from the plantation the same day, despite having worked there as sharecropper and timekeeper for eighteen years. What happened was that I got home and my children told me the plantation owner, Mr Marlow, had been looking for me. He arrived soon after and said, 'Fannie Lou, you have been to the courthouse to register. We are not ready for this yet in Mississippi. Take it back by tomorrow morning, or you will have to leave.' I was fired that day and have not had a job since. People shot up the houses of black people nearby because of this. Two girls got shot. In 1963 I was on a bus home from a meeting when some of the others were arrested for trying to eat in a segregated restaurant. I got out to help, so I was arrested too. They took us to the jail. I could hear beating and screaming.

*Then they came for me. They took me into a cell. There were two Negro prisoners. They gave one of them a long heavy **blackjack**, made me lie on the other bunk and had him beat me. Then they had the other one beat me, while the first one sat on my feet.*

Fannie Lou Hamer later said:
If you just stand there and don't lash back you can find a real human being in a lot of people. I've been part of a non-violent revolution. I'd say, 'As long as you stand with your feet on my neck you got to stand in a ditch too. You move, then I can get out. I want us to both get out of the ditch.'

Things to do

1 Why did black people choose to use non-violent methods of protest in the 1950s and 1960s?

2 What does Source A tell you about attitudes at the time?

3 Read Fannie Lou Hamer's story.

   a Why do you think the people whose houses were 'shot up' did not go to the police for help?

   b What do you think Fannie Lou meant by her comment that begins 'As long as you stand with your feet on my neck'?

The Little Rock Nine, Arkansas, September 1957

Little Rock was progressive, for a southern town. It had de-segregated some libraries and parks, even the police force. No one was prepared for the white reaction to the move to **integrate** nine black children into the High School. On the first day, the Governor of Arkansas, Orval Faubus, sent in state troops to keep the children out at gunpoint. Two weeks later, after the President had told Faubus to let them in, the children were smuggled into the school by the city police. When word got out that they were in the school, a riot broke out. The police had to smuggle them out.

The children were finally taken into the school by government troops. For the first week they were taken in and out by soldiers and had a personal escort all day. But when the troops withdrew, the children's troubles began. They were ignored or taunted by the teachers and students. But they knew that if they fought back they would be expelled. They were in real danger of being hurt, even killed, in the early riots. Afterwards they were still in danger. One of them, Melba Patillo, was nearly blinded when a chemical was thrown at her.

ERNEST GREEN

Most people didn't believe the President would use force to get us in. At first it was pretty quiet. The segregationists were waiting for us to get tired and go. We didn't. They came back. Then the troops went. All hell broke lose. It was trench warfare. They'd taunt you in the corridors, try to trip you, throw ink at you. There were water guns too. You'd get phone calls at night, saying they'd have acid in the water guns and squirt it in our faces. You'd be crazy not to be scared. But we had to go. And we had to be non-violent.

They picked on the girls most. This bunch of kids were really after Minnie. One was like a small dog, snapping at her all the time. He just had to figure out how many different ways he could say 'nigger'. He touched Minnie's last nerve. He was in front of her in the lunch line. I could see it coming, but before I could say, 'Minnie, don't do it. Forget him...' she had dumped her bowl of chilli on his head. It just rolled down his face. The school board used the incident to expel her. In school students passed round little printed cards: 'One down, eight to go'.

Some white kids tried to be friendly, but they really got it. They got hate mail and calls. We got through with family support and each other.

ELIZABETH ECKFORD

Elizabeth Eckford arrived alone on the first day of school. Having passed through an angry mob of parents, she was turned away by an armed guard. She later said:

There were lots of black kids doing what we did. We weren't unusual, but we got the attention. We couldn't fight back or we'd be expelled, which might mean the end of integration. It was a daily torment for us and our parents. But we had to make integration work.

The Children's Crusade, Birmingham, Alabama, May 1963

Birmingham, Alabama, was chosen as the target for a huge campaign for civil rights, which lasted for weeks. It included marches, sit-ins and the Children's Crusade. Children marched towards the white area of town, knowing they would be arrested and put in jail. The police ran out of police vans and had to take the children to jail in school buses. By 4 p.m., 959 children were in jail.

The next day more children marched. Bull Connor, the man in charge of the police, brought in firemen armed with water hoses and policemen with dogs. After three days, more than 2000 people were in jail, mostly children. Many more were in hospital. Pictures of children as young as six being soaked by fire hoses, beaten by police and set on by dogs shocked the world. Birmingham had to start to de-segregate.

Source A

Three accounts of the Children's Crusade.

Audrey Hendricks: I was nine when I marched. I was arrested. They took me to a room where five, six white men questioned me. It was a small room. I was scared what they would do to me. I was only little. I was in jail seven days.

Mary Gadson: There were hundreds of us. Bull Connor said they'd set the dogs on us. They had fire hoses too. That water was strong. It could knock you down. I got wet and almost bitten.

Myrna Carter: On the Sunday march, they were waiting at Memorial Park. The firemen were there with hoses and the police with dogs on leashes. The police thought it was funny to let the dogs lunge at us, then pull back. We were scared, but we carried on. And we stood there. When Bull Connor ordered them to turn the fire hoses on, they didn't, even when he swore.

Source B

Marchers caught by a fire hose.

Things to do

1 Choose either Little Rock or the Children's Crusade.

   a Write a paragraph about it for a newspaper that is in favour of segregation.
   b Write a paragraph about it for a newspaper that is against segregation.

2 Imagine you are one of the children who took part. Write a diary entry about how taking part made you feel.

3 What do the Little Rock incident and the Children's Crusade tell us about life in the United States at this time?

It was a constant struggle to make a difference to white attitudes. Millions of people were involved every day – old and young, famous and ordinary. Here are just a few of them.

MARTIN LUTHER KING

Martin Luther King went south in 1954 as a Baptist minister and civil rights leader. He took a big part in the civil rights campaigns of the 1950s and 1960s. He made speeches, led marches and got people organised. He believed in non-violent protest. It was, he said, *important to make changes in the hearts and minds of white people, not to break their bodies.*

When his home was bombed by whites in 1956, he told a crowd of armed supporters: *If you have weapons, take them home. 'He who lives by the sword, will perish by the sword.' Remember that is what Jesus said. We are not advocating violence. We want to love our enemies. Be good to them, that is what we must live by. We must meet hate with love.* King won the Nobel Peace Prize in 1964. In 1968 he was assassinated. The third Monday in January is now Martin Luther King Day, a public holiday in the USA.

Source A

Myrna Carter, who went on the Birmingham Children's Crusade in 1963, heard Martin Luther King speak.

At first I thought I was going to be afraid, but the fear went. Dr King's voice had a power like no one else's. It wasn't that we worshipped him. We didn't. He wasn't like that at all. But he could somehow make you leap without realising that you were leaping.

Source B

The woman in the centre of this picture is Septima Clark. She taught thousands of black people who could not read or write how to pass the tests they had to take to be allowed to vote. Without her help, these black people would not have had a say in elections.

Source C

In 1964, there were black demonstrations in the North.
Government troops helped some black movements in the South,
but they were not on the side of black people at this demonstration
in Cambridge, Massachusetts.

ARLEN CARR

*In 1964 we won our court case to de-segregate schools. I felt
so good. When I started at Lanier High School there were
thirteen of us. They told us to come on the second day, after
school had started. They walked us from the principal's office
to our classrooms. We were all in separate classes. You know
how kids are on the first day of school – talking, making a
lot of noise. The principal opened the door and said to my
teacher, 'He's in your class.' I stepped in and the kids saw
me – you could have heard a pin drop.*

*I'll never forget how you could be walking down the hall,
and they'd just part. The first time, I was a little intimidated,
but then I felt like a king – the waters parting for the black
kids. That's fine with me. Got no problem with that. After a
while their attitude was: 'Well, they're here, we gotta accept
them. Got to go to school, so let's make the best of it.' We did
make some friends, mostly from the air force base, where the
kids had lived in different parts of the country and been
around black kids more. Senior year I asked a white guy to
sign my yearbook. I had known him from tenth grade, we
were pretty good friends. He wrote that he had been a bigot
and hated black people. Now he realised that people were
people, black or white. Meeting me and knowing me had
changed him. He ended with 'We shall overcome'.*

Things to do

1 Choose one of the people
   described or photographed
   on these pages.

   Write a paragraph to
   explain how they made a
   difference to the way black
   people were treated.

2 Use evidence from pages
   40–55 to say whether you
   agree or disagree with the
   following statements:

   a 'One person, even an
      important one, can't
      make a difference
      to things.'

   b 'Black people should
      not just have let people
      pour things on them,
      beat them up and bomb
      them. They should have
      fought back.'

   c 'Black people should have
      moved out of the South.
      They were never going
      to get equality there.'

In 1963, Martin Luther King led a huge protest march to the US capital, Washington. The President, John F. Kennedy, said: *Now the time has come for the nation to keep its promise. Those who do nothing are inviting shame as well as violence.* But progress was painfully slow. And the price of equality was paid by black people and their white supporters, who were persecuted, beaten up and even killed. People began to say it was time to change tactics: to take black rights by force and to fight back if they were attacked.

MALCOLM X

One of the first people to speak out in favour of stronger action was Malcolm X. His real name was Little; 'X' stands for all the names taken from black slaves. As a schoolboy, Malcolm told his teacher he wanted to be a lawyer. His teacher was shocked. *That's not a job for a nigger*, he said. From then on, Malcolm felt education was not the way; it taught black people to expect too little. He became a Black Muslim. Black Muslims followed the Islamic religion and said black people should be self-sufficient and proud to be black. Malcolm X was assassinated in 1965.

Source A

Malcolm X spoke to students from Mississippi in New York City in 1964.

How do you think I feel to have to tell you, 'We, my generation, sat around like blocks of wood while the whole world fought for human rights. You've been born into a society where you still have that fight'? What did we do, who went before you? I'll tell you what we did. We did nothing. Don't you make the same mistake. Don't try to be friends with somebody who's depriving you of your rights. They are not your friends. They're your enemies. Treat them like that. Fight and you'll get your freedom.

Source B

Julius Lester wrote about Malcolm X in 1968. The title of his book, *Look out Whitey! Black Power's Gonna Get Your Momma!* summed up the fears that had driven some white people to racism.

More than anyone else, Malcolm X was responsible for growing awareness and **militancy** among black people. His clear words cut the chains on black minds like a giant blowtorch. He did not want to awake the conscience of America about black rights. He knew America had no conscience.

Source C

Not everyone joined the more violent groups. The civil rights movement carried on its peaceful protests. The result of this march from Selma, Alabama, to Montgomery in March 1965 was the Voting Rights Act of August 1965. This gave the government greater powers to force states to allow black people to vote. This seemed like a huge victory. But the next day, at a march in Montgomery, marchers were beaten up by the police.

The photo looks peaceful, but the story is not. These people lost their home and jobs in Greene County, Alabama, when they registered to vote in 1966. Four days after the photo was taken, the pregnant woman began to have her baby. The local white hospital turned her away. She bled to death before they could reach another hospital.

Riots

Even when peaceful protest won government support, it was impossible to enforce black rights in many places. Often the law enforcers, the soldiers and police, were the ones beating up black people. More and more black people became angry. The words 'race riot' had meant violence against black people. Now they were as likely to mean violence by them. Martin Luther King said: *Everyone underestimated the amount of rage the Negroes were feeling but holding back and the amount of prejudice most white people were hiding.*

Things get worse

Violent protest came from many groups, some more extreme than others. They brought back the Marcus Garvey slogan 'Black is Beautiful' and a new one: 'Black Power'. Unplanned violence also came from ordinary people. As violence spread, the peaceful black protests became less newsworthy. The press lapped up black violence, while ignoring white violence. The image of black people as out of control, which many white people had always believed in, was supported almost daily by newspapers and television.

Source E

Martin Luther King was murdered three months after he made this speech to the Press in 1968.

I don't know if you realise it, but you are driving non-violent people like me into saying more and more militant things. If we don't say what you want we don't get on the news. Who does? The militants. By doing this you are, first, presenting militant black leaders as civil rights leaders. And secondly, you're making violence the way to publicise our cause.

Things to do

1 a How did black protest change during the 1960s?
 b Why?
 c Why did some blacks feel the new approach was wrong?
 d What did Julius Lester (Source B) mean when he talked about 'the chains on black minds'?

2 Look at Source D and read the caption. Were all, or any, of the following people responsible for the pregnant woman's death:

 a the people who took away their jobs
 b her family for registering to vote
 c the hospital staff at the white hospital, for turning her away
 d the Alabama state government
 e the white people of Alabama?

The first large-scale riot broke out in Los Angeles in the summer of 1965. It set a pattern. The summers of 1966, 1967 and 1968 were full of rioting. Much of it was in big cities such as Los Angeles, Detroit, Newark and Chicago. The rioters had many reasons for taking to the streets:

- **Political:** Black people still had more rights on paper than in real life. There were now black people in the government, but there were not enough.
- **Social:** Black people still had to live in the worst housing. The areas where they lived did not always have the same level of services (rubbish collection, street lighting and so on) as better-off, mainly white areas. Many black children were still in segregated schools, simply because their local schools were in mainly black areas. These schools tended to get less money and equipment. Black people, especially young black men, were regularly harassed by the police for no reason.
- **Economic:** Black people were still expected to do the worst jobs, the 'Negro jobs' of the 1920s. They were still not paid the same wages.

Not all bad?

Around this time, black people were breaking all kinds of barriers: to be the first black person in a law firm, the first black executive in a business or the first black mayor of a town. But these individuals still had to make a big effort to get the job and then be accepted. The riots broke out mainly in poor areas, where lots of black people were crammed together and were obviously not treated as equal to whites.

Source A

Howard Morris, Director of the National Urban League, went to Newark in 1967.

I was visiting family and friends. We were out on the porch. About three police cars came round the corner. With no warning they opened fire on us. They said there was a sniper on the roof. But they were firing at ground level. My stepfather was killed. My brother was badly wounded. And I realised that no matter how well the Negro does, there's still white prejudice. I had two degrees. I work with white people and have white friends. But it counted for nothing then. I was lumped in with rioters, I was black. The riots were a good excuse to shoot up any group of Negroes.

Troops patrol the streets of Los Angeles after the riots of 1965.

Source B

Buildings burning during riots in Los Angeles in July 1992.

Recent events

In 1992 there was more rioting in Los Angeles and other major cities. The issues were the same as they had been in the 1960s. There had been no noticeable improvements to living conditions.

Source D

A young black woman spoke about the 1992 Los Angeles riots on TV in 1996.

It was pretty scary. All the burning, all the rage. My kids are pretty young, you know. It was hard to explain why their neighbours were reacting this way. But then, it's been hard to explain why we have to live like this, too. Rubbish on the streets, their homes and schools all beat up and not fixed. So I had to sort of explain and tell them, 'We are tired of this. We are angry.'

Source E

Jean Carey Bond wrote to the *New York Times* in 1994 about the kind of behaviour that drove black people to despair.

When my son, who is in his 20s now, was a teenager, he was walking home after a school event when a police car screeched to a halt in front of him. Its doors flew open and four white cops jumped out, guns drawn. They threw him up against a wall, patted him down and grilled him, a gun at his head all the while. Fortunately for my son, a white classmate was passing and identified him to the cops. It seems a mugging had occurred in the area, and my son fitted the description of the mugger – meaning my son was black.

Source F

A letter to African-American voters written by the black politician Ron Brown in 1990.

In 1964 Fannie Lou Hamer fought to get just one seat at the Democratic National Convention. Now I am Chairman of the Party. We have a black Governor, black Congressmen. That's a long way in a short time. We have opportunities our parents never had.

But one in three blacks live in poverty. Many more live in areas with poor schools, high crime, drug abuse, too few jobs, too little hope. A recent study showed that at the current rate of progress for black equality:

- it will be 2058 before black men earn as much as white men in the same job
- it will be 2154 before there are not more blacks living in poverty than whites.

Things to do

Use the sources on these pages to answer the questions below.

a Why did riots break out in American cities in the 1960s?

b Did riots break out in the early 1990s for the same reasons?

c Does this mean that black people had made no progress between the 1960s and the 1990s?

Have things improved for black people in the USA? Is equality still as far off as ever? It depends on who you look at and where you look. The last few pages have looked at the very real reasons that black people have to be angry. Now let's look at some reasons to be glad.

Source A

John H. Johnson started publishing the magazine *Negro Digest* in November 1942.

We'd just come off government aid and I got a loan to start *Negro Digest*. In November 1945 I started *Ebony*. In November 1951 I started *Jet*. In other Novembers, other years, I started up black fashions and black cosmetics. Today I own the biggest black-based business in America. I'm involved in the running of lots of other big companies.

Sport

Sport is one area where black people have always led the field. Black boxers and baseball, basketball and American football players are all at the top of their sports in the USA. Black athletes, male and female, regularly win many medals at the Olympic Games.

SPIKE LEE

Spike Lee, a writer, director and film-maker, makes films that are relevant to black people, especially young black people. He said: *Film is a powerful medium. It can influence how millions of people think. It can make you rich. Don't fall for junk like 'You gotta be struck by lightning to be a film-maker'.*

Source B

Television programmes now regularly feature black families. One of the most popular children's TV shows in the USA and Britain is 'Sister Sister', which stars black twins.

Three ways to look at the history of black people in the Americas.

We've come a long way. Black people are not slaves. We have rights. We can vote, have an education. We have important jobs in all areas of life, from politics to the media. There are famous black American film stars, basketball players, writers, politicians.

We've had a huge struggle to get any rights at all over this time. And we've got far more rights on paper than in real life. We are most likely to live in slum housing, most likely to go to bad schools, less likely to be employed. We were struggling against racism and fear at the beginning. We're struggling against them now.

We are struggling. But we are getting places. History shows life in America hasn't been fair to black people. It isn't fair now. But it is a fact that we are not going to get equality easily, even though it is clearly right that we should. Maybe separation is the answer.

Things to do

Think about what you have learned in this study about the struggle of black people for equality. Now say which of these three speakers you agree with most. Why?

blackjack a club with a heavy, leaded end.

boycotted refused to visit places for social and political reasons.

Constitution a set of rules and ideas which a government uses to rule the country.

cotton gin a machine for separating cotton from the seeds.

Federal government the government which made the laws that had to be obeyed all over the country.

Freedmen's Bureau an organisation set up by the **Federal government** to make sure that the anti-slavery laws were enforced.

indentured servants people who signed a contract to work for a number of years for whoever paid for them to travel to America. They could not leave during this time.

integrate to mix together black and white people where they had previously been **segregated**.

Islamic to do with the religion of the Muslims.

lynchings murdering people for a supposed crime without a trial, usually by hanging.

migrants people who do not live in a fixed place, but live wherever they can find work or food.

militancy aggressive action in support of a particular cause.

overseers people who overlook and supervise the work of others.

plantations estates on which tobacco and cotton and other products are grown.

planter the manager of a **plantation**.

racial prejudice the belief that one race or colour of people is superior to another, and the unfair behaviour that this attitude leads to.

segregation the enforced separation of different races and colours in society.

sharecropping a farmer giving part of their crops as rent for the land on which the crops are grown, instead of money.

tanning yards places where animal hides are turned into leather.

voodoo the use of and belief in religious witchcraft and magic.

INDEX